Plants for shade

Plants for shade

Andrew Mikolajski

LONDON, NEW YORK, MUNICH,
MELBOURNE, DELHI

SENIOR EDITOR Zia Allaway
ACTING SENIOR DESIGNER Rachael Smith
PROJECT EDITOR Emma Callery
PROJECT ART EDITOR Alison Shackleton
MANAGING EDITOR Anna Kruger
MANAGING ART EDITOR Alison Donovan
DTP DESIGNER Louise Waller
PICTURE RESEARCH Lucy Claxton,
Richard Dabb, Mel Watson
PRODUCTION CONTROLLER Rebecca Short

PHOTOGRAPHY Peter Anderson

First American Edition, 2007

Published in the United States by
DK Publishing, 375 Hudson Street,
New York, NY 10014

07 08 09 10 11   10 9 8 7 6 5 4 3 2 1

A Cataloging-in-Publication record for this book is
available from the Library of Congress.

ISBN-13: 978-0-7566-2693-8

ISBN-10: 0-7566-2693-5

DK books are available at special discounts for bulk
purchases for sales promotions, premiums, fund-raising, or
educational use. For details, contact: DK Publishing Special
Markets, 375 Hudson Street, New York, NY 10014 or
SpecialSales@dk.com

Reproduced by Colourscan, Singapore
Printed and bound in Singapore by Star Standard

Discover more at
www.dk.com

Contents

Benefits of shade

Given the choice between a shady yard and a sunny one, most experienced gardeners would unhesitatingly opt for the latter. But in doing so, they are overlooking the beauty of cool green spaces bathed in dappled shade. Even a garden in deep shade has its charms, especially when adorned with richly textured foliage plants. The design ideas in this chapter show you how to get the most from your shady yard, and how the sun's dynamic quality—changing from hour to hour, and day to day—can be used to create an exciting play of shadows and light.

The beauty of dappled shade

The light shade cast by deciduous trees is always beguiling. Constantly changing, the quality of the shade alters from day to day as leaves unfurl in spring, and even from moment to moment as the foliage dances in the breeze.

Pictures clockwise from top left

Sparkling reflections Water is a mesmerizing presence in a garden, drawing all down toward its reflective surface. This Islamic-inspired formal pool mirrors the airy leaf canopy of an elegant stand of birches (*Betula*), while the water itself is unplanted.

Cool journey A path that leads from a shady area into the sun beckons you on toward the light. Here, the richly planted borders, filled with an informal mix of shade-loving shrubs and perennials chosen for their flowers or architectural form, encourage you to take your time.

Lawn mosaic Grass shaded by an overhanging tree makes an ideal spot for a summer picnic. For a green sward beneath deciduous trees, make sure you choose a seed mixture or sod type that tolerates shade.

Shy beauty Of all the plants that thrive in dappled shade, perhaps the best are the hellebores (*Helleborus*). Evergreen, and largely disease-resistant, they are the perennial of choice for late winter and early spring interest. The cup-shaped flowers show a range of colors from cream, white, and pink, to cherry red and blackish purple. Some are dramatically flecked and spotted.

Contrasts within deep shade

Quite a few plants will thrive in deep shade, but some blue-sky thinking is needed design-wise, as shade usually limits flowering potential. Your color range is inevitably restricted, but any flowers, while rare, will gleam like jewels. Aim for a good mix of evergreen and deciduous plants, with some strong architectural subjects for impact.

Pictures clockwise from top left

Woodland glade This planting looks very naturalistic, but has been carefully contrived to exploit the possibilities. Ferns, always a sound choice provided the ground stays reasonably moist, and foxgloves (*Digitalis purpurea*) make a winning combination. Here, the white form glimmers in the shadows. The bugle (*Ajuga reptans*) in the foreground has spikes of blue summer flowers like mini pagodas. White- and pink-flowered forms are also available.

Shady enclosure An enclosed courtyard may receive little, if any, direct sunlight, but that apparent problem has been turned into an advantage here. In a closed, damp environment, mosses will proliferate, and their presence is a positive ornament to the traditional herringbone brick paving. Hostas, ferns, and ivies complete the scene. A word of warning: moss can become slippery underfoot, especially during wet weather, and slugs will thrive in these conditions almost as much as the mosses.

Cool resting place Less is more in this sophisticated urban garden, and the shade-loving planting has been chosen to act as a foil to the beautifully crafted oak bench, the main point of interest here. It invites you to sit and pause a while beneath a leafy canopy to appreciate the contrast in foliage shape and texture around you. The large-leaved plants give a subtropical feel.

Bright highlights Among the plants that will flower in deep shade, the hardy cyclamen (*Cyclamen* spp.) are among the most beautiful, diminutive in size but breathtaking where they are planted *en masse*. Flower colors include many shades of pink, carmine red, and, perhaps most desirable, white. The majority have marbled leaves, which add to their appeal.

Shade throughout the day

Shade is not a constant and changes throughout the day, as well as from season to season. In winter, the sun is lower, so shadows are longer during the day, while in summer, light floods the garden for much longer. This courtyard garden shows just how dramatically light and shade can vary in a single day.

Pictures counterclockwise from top of page

Morning The position of this house and the low boundary wall to the east means that on a clear day, a slice of north-facing garden is flooded with early morning light. Morning sun can be strong, but the temperature is likely to be low, especially following a cool night. The boundary walls that cast shade also provide shelter, so the deck is a pleasant sitting area for breakfast.

Noon Within a few hours, however, the sun is well on its way across the sky. The house is casting a solid shadow over half of the graveled area lying beyond the deck, which will now not see any more direct sunlight until the following morning. From here on, the potted plants on the deck will be in shade. While this area is cool, the back of the garden has become a sun-trap and the heat there may be intense—light-colored stonework both reflects light and holds warmth, suiting the Mediterranean herbs that have been planted there.

Evening Later on, at cocktail hour, no direct light reaches the garden at all. It has become a shady, cool retreat, welcome if the day has been a hot one. The hard landscaping and gravel emit a residual warmth that will encourage you to linger there even after sundown.

Late summer The sun is much higher in summer and shadows are generally shorter, especially around noon. Even though this garden is predominantly shady, there is still enough indirect light to make it a pleasant area for relaxation and outdoor entertaining. Predominantly green-leaved plants have been chosen, as these are generally tolerant of lower light levels. Grasses, both in pots and planted through a membrane under the gravel, are good choices and look attractive over a long period.

Shade throughout the year

The changing angle of the sun as the globe tilts on its annual transit means that gardens receive markedly different levels of light from season to season. Assessing the sunlight your yard receives at different times will help you plan your plantings throughout the year.

Pictures from bottom left
Spring Once past the equinox, the date when daylight and darkness are equally balanced, the amount of light starts to increase dramatically and shadows begin to shorten as the sun climbs higher in the sky. Most deciduous trees and shrubs, and climbers trained on freestanding trellises or arbors, have some time to go before they develop their full complement of leaves, allowing low-growing plants to take advantage of the filtered light beneath them.

Summer This is a season of great contrast in the garden. Around the longest day, and for about six to eight weeks afterward, the sun can beat down with a fierce heat. At noon, it may appear to be virtually overhead, and shadows are short. Trees and shrubs are in full leaf, casting pools of dense shade, and tall perennials will be casting shade too. Solid structures, such as arbors, offer a cool retreat at this time.

Fall Most gardeners, and not just the fruit-growers, love this season. Back at a lower angle, the sun casts longer shadows, and as leaves turn color, shrivel, and drop, deciduous trees and shrubs cast an enchanting dappled shade. This is a time for getting gardening jobs done quickly, as every day there are fewer hours of light.

Winter This is a quiet time, when most gardens have a bare, open look. There will almost certainly be some clear, cloudless days among the gloomy ones, but shadows are long, and some areas of the garden that enjoy sunshine in summer may now receive no direct light at all. If this really gets you down, include plenty of winter-interest plants to look forward to.

Shade cast by solid structures

In many gardens, shade is a given—cast either by elements outside the garden or by boundary walls and screens designed to create a private, relaxing space. Here are some imaginative ways to transform this perceived negative into a positive situation.

Pictures clockwise from far left

External influences Neighboring houses and other buildings cast solid shade and create a sense of enclosure that can be threatening or comforting, depending on how you look at it. This garden borrows the neighboring house and a boundary wall to create a sort of Italianate grotto, a refuge of lush leaves and a playful water feature.

Wooden boundaries Approaching any problem in strictly design terms will often yield a stylish solution. Here, the fence panels themselves seem to have dictated the planting, the horizontals reflected in the massed ferns, contrasted with the bold uprights of the birches (*Betula*) and foxgloves (*Digitalis*).

Wall coverings A wall at the end of a garden, or perhaps of an outbuilding or adjoining garage, can easily be enlivened with climbing plants, a good many of which will flower as readily in shade as they would in sun. Some of the climbing roses are shade-tolerant—this one is 'Kathleen Harrop'—and will provide a sumptuous display of fragrant pale pink blooms in the summer.

Asian style An important aspect of garden design is integration—the sense that all the elements in any given space belong with each other. These bamboo panels used as screening give an Asian, almost subtropical feel, and this is reflected in the choice of plants. Large-leaved hostas and ferns are made for shade.

Shade cast by plantings

Depending on the type of plant, the shadows they cast vary. Evergreen trees and shrubs that achieve great bulk create shade as deep as any wall, while airy deciduous types are more mercurial, filtering the light in spring and whenever the air moves, and casting denser pools of darkness once in full leaf.

Pictures clockwise from top left

Canopied courtyard Low hedging is ideal for defining an area without cutting it off from the rest of the garden. In the winter, when the birches (*Betula*) are bare, you look over it to the semiformal planting beyond. When in full leaf in summer, the area beneath the canopy becomes a cool, inviting place for an al fresco meal. The birches have the advantage of shining white bark, but there are some attractive alternatives with beautiful trunks and stems. Rowans (*Sorbus*), lindens (*Tilia*), *Populus* x *jackii* 'Aurora', and the Indian bean tree (*Catalpa bignonioides*) are among their number.

Cool waters Where the ground is reliably moist, bog plants will grow lushly, although some are suitable only for larger gardens. The gunnera in the middle of this planting has the biggest leaves of any hardy plant, extending to 6 ft (2 m) or more across on stems almost as tall as an average man. It dies back in winter. These moisture-lovers are backed by sky-scraping willows and other trees, which cast shade over this cool oasis in summer.

Jungle trail There are certain plants that, while perfectly hardy, seem to have an exotic bearing and can be used to give almost any garden a tropical look. The tree fern (*Dicksonia antarctica*) and Chusan palm (*Trachycarpus fortunei*) are shade-tolerant jungly plants, their fronds keeping cool the more versatile grasses, ferns, and candelabra primulas in this streamside planting. As with many shade plantings, green is the predominant color here, enlivened by flecks of orange, purple, and pink.

Shade cast by planting *continued*

Pictures clockwise from left

Fiery lights Red-hot pokers (*Kniphofia*) are South Africans that are normally thought of as sun-lovers, but they will also flower well in light shade—what they don't like is excessive rain in winter. They are the dominant feature of this warm scheme and are shaded by the butter yellow leaves of *Ulmus glabra* 'Lutescens' and flanked by golden privet (*Ligustrum ovalifolium* 'Aureum'). Lady's mantle (*Alchemilla mollis*) in the foreground grows anywhere. In a more limited space, use a smaller poker such as 'Little Maid'.

Flower fusion It can be difficult to find plants to put next to a hedge as it casts heavy shade and dries out the soil close to it, but *Rosa rugosa* is a tough, tolerant rose that puts up with both conditions. Unlike some other shrub roses, it makes a pleasing mound covered with attractive leaves, and large, deliciously fragrant pink or white summer flowers. Hardy geraniums are good companions, and there is just enough sun to encourage the silver-leaved *Brachyglottis* to the fore to flower.

Subtle elegance Any shady border is going to be predominantly green at some stage, but can still have a dynamic quality with the right plants. Drifts of the same plant are often more impressive than a lot of different ones, as demonstrated here by the carpet of pulmonarias, a good alternative to hostas in a slug-infested garden. These are shaded by a backdrop of shrubs and spiky irises, while the boxwood ball adds texture and more height.

Rose screen Some climbing and rambling roses will tolerate shade, or, if trained over an arbor or other freestanding structure, can be used to cast shade. *Rosa* 'Veilchenblau' is shade-tolerant and valued for the clusters of violet-blue flowers—an unusual color for a rose—that it pours out generously in early summer.

Managing shade

Shady gardens are beautiful and calming spaces, and this chapter shows how those with a sunny site can create a cool oasis filled with plants they would otherwise be unable to grow. At the other end of the scale, a really dark, dank area can be oppressive and restrict your planting choices. If this is your problem, discover how to lighten and transform your garden into a more desirable space. There are also tips on choosing a lawn or hard surface for your yard, and information on different soil types and how to improve them.

Creating shade with walls, fences, and screens

It's easy to overlook the desirability of shade, until the sun comes beating down in summer and you long for a cool retreat. Here are some simple ways of creating shade without sacrificing plants' needs for light.

Beautiful bamboo

You can disguise an ugly fence with bamboo screening, usually sold on the roll or in panels. This product suits the Asian-style planting here. A shade-tolerant living bamboo has been planted in front of it, and the golden yellow lilies are in a glazed Asian container. Alternatives to this type of screening include woven hazel or willow, both of which suit a more rustic scheme.

Wall style The shade afforded by a wall has great potential. Here, it has been painted white to raise the light level to suit the sun-loving pelargoniums, and the lobelias make a great contrasting trailer. When grown in small pots, some plants that generally prefer sun do better in some shade, where the potting mix doesn't dry out so quickly.

Cool arbor This leafy seat has a dual purpose. At some times of day it can be a sun-trap, while at other times it offers a shady retreat to escape the sun's harshest rays. The wisteria loses its leaves in winter, allowing more light to filter through. Remember, too, that solid structures such as this will cast shade onto adjacent plantings.

Dappled shade

A trellis screen is useful for dividing up the garden while at the same time offering tantalizing glimpses of what lies beyond. The golden hop (*Humulus lupulus* 'Aureus') is a perennial climber that dies back to below the ground every year, so in winter you will be able to look straight through the trellis. In summer, it creates a sense of enclosure. The plant itself needs light to bring out the rich yellow in the leaf, but at the same time does a good job of casting shade over the perennials planted at its feet.

Too hot to handle

In a very open site, you may feel the need to create shade on a temporary basis. A canopy or sail such as this one is easily erected, assuming you have had some practice in pitching a tent. Leave it *in situ* during a hot spell or move it around the garden where required. The plants will benefit from shelter from hot sun just as much as you do, particularly if they are the kind that scorch easily. If you accidentally leave the canopy out in the rain, dry it thoroughly before storing to prevent mold from developing.

Creating shade with trees and shrubs

Making a shady area with plants is easy, and although trees and shrubs take a few years to mature, your patience will be rewarded by the effects they create.

Woodland feel If you love being among trees but have only a small yard to play with, plant just a few small, slim trees, such as birches (*Betula*). The dappled shade they cast also allows you to plant beneath them.

Leafy tunnels Trees trained over to form an archway or tunnel can be used to shade a pathway that leads from one area of the garden to another. Hazel (*Corylus*), laburnum, and beech (*Fagus*) are all suitable.

Planting combinations Use smaller-growing plants to shade one another. Here, a shade-loving heuchera is sheltering in the embrace of a hebe and a yew ball, while the plants to the fore are in sun.

Evergreen screen This old statue seems to have caught something of the somber mood cast by an evergreen yew (*Taxus*) hedge, but white campanulas lighten the gloom. Yew grows much faster than most gardeners realize.

Seasonal shade Mixing evergreen and deciduous plants has a dynamic effect. The shade cast by deciduous ones varies through the year, while evergreens maintain a solid presence. Clipping both types creates a sculptural effect.

Lightening shady sites

It's quite possible to bring light—or at least a semblance of light—to predominantly shady sites with a few basic techniques. Think conceptually, not literally.

Painting walls white A white wall reflects light and appears to glow even if it receives no direct sun at all. Brighten an enclosed courtyard with a lick of paint, using white or another pale color.

Whiter shade of pale White objects always appear to be bigger than they actually are because of the light they reflect. *Rodgersia aesculifolia* has pale, pinkish white flowers in early summer that match the gleaming bark of the birches (*Betula*) that they are planted beneath.

Bright pots It sounds obvious, but using white or light-colored pots will brighten up a shady patio. It makes sense to use glazed terra cotta, which is easy to keep clean—painted terra cotta rapidly develops green algal patches and white plastic does not age well.

Lifting canopies

It's a given that tall trees and shrubs cast shade, but sometimes they have to be retained to provide necessary privacy. However, you can cut out some lower branches to allow light through, giving you the best of both worlds. For larger branches, use a pruning saw and make two cuts to prevent the stem from ripping and damaging the plant.

First, cut under the branch, sawing just halfway through. Then make another cut above it, so that the two cuts meet.

Removing the lower branches and some from the tree's crown allows the perennials below to receive sufficient light for flowering.

Lawns and alternative surfaces

All gardens need open areas for relaxation and entertaining, but different surfaces suit different needs and styles. Choose the one that's right for you and your garden.

Shades of green Grass is always soft underfoot and is the surface of choice for a rustic or informal garden. In an enclosed site, it's essential to choose a seed mix or sod type that is shade-tolerant.

Paving Ideal for any part of the garden that sees heavy traffic, paving is a great option for shade. Watch out for the growth of mosses and lichens between pavers—when wet, they can make the nimblest gardener lose their footing.

Decking Wooden decking can look very sophisticated, especially in an urban garden that makes no reference to an outlying landscape. Since it's less durable than paving, it inevitably has a shorter life span.

Gravel Few gardeners would have trouble laying gravel—simply spread it over a weed-suppressing fabric. Gravel is ideal for shady areas, since it doesn't become slippery when wet and reflects light into the gloom.

Using shady sites for houseplants

It's worth remembering that many houseplants originate in the rainforest where light levels are poor, which explains why they can do well in shady sites outdoors in summer when night temperatures don't drop too low.

Using pesticides and fungicides Plants grown indoors are susceptible to a range of pests and diseases. The wider range of insect life outdoors can help control certain pests, such as aphids, and the improved air circulation prevents fungi from taking hold. However, if your houseplants do succumb to pests and diseases, it's often easier to apply pesticides outdoors, during still weather, when the product will not be blown off the leaves.

Mixing houseplants with summer bedding Valued largely for their foliage, houseplants can make dramatic and unexpected additions to bedding schemes and outdoor container displays. Spider plants (*Chlorophytum*) and trailing tradescantias are particularly good candidates. You will need to acclimatize the plants first. Put them outdoors for increasingly longer periods during the daytime from late spring onward to toughen the delicate leaves. Choose a sheltered site for your plants, where the temperature range is narrower than in the open garden and the plants are protected from strong winds.

Encouraging cymbidiums to flower Among the evergreen orchids that are commonly grown as houseplants, cymbidiums are unusual in that they need fluctuating temperatures at the end of the growing season to encourage them to flower the following year. The simplest way to achieve this is to place the plants outdoors in a shady, sheltered spot during summer and early fall, when nighttime temperatures are starting to drop. Bring them back indoors before the first frosts. Fat flower spikes will subsequently emerge around the base of the plant in late winter, producing quantities of showy, exotic flowers from mid-spring onward.

Creating a beautiful display on a shady terrace
Plants in containers—including houseplants—can lead
a wandering life, being moved around the garden and in
and out of doors. This subtropical-looking scheme of
hardy and tender plants brings interest to a shady area.

Improving soil in shady sites

Soil management is an important part of gardening. Keeping the soil in good heart is a rewarding process that allows plants to perform to their optimum.

Soil conditioner Garden compost that you make yourself is the very best soil conditioner. It improves the structure of soil, opening up air pockets in heavy clay and binding loose sand into crumbs.

Making your own For the best compost, use as wide a range of material as possible—raw vegetable peelings, overripe fruit, wilted vegetables, annual weeds, grass cuttings, eggshells, shredded newspaper, and cardboard ripped into small pieces. Conifer prunings and the leaves of evergreens don't break down readily. Human urine—assuming you can devise a discreet means of delivery—and farmyard manure are good activators. Stack in loose layers in a composting bin. Ideally, the pile should be turned every two or three weeks to speed up the process. The compost is ready to use when brown, crumbly, and sweet-smelling, and when individual constituents can no longer be identified—usually after about 12 weeks, sometimes longer.

Using compost You can apply compost in a number of ways. If you are making a new border, dig over the ground first, then fork in the compost by the bucketful. If you are introducing new plants into an existing border, work in a few handfuls of compost at the base of each planting hole. Compost can also be spread over the ground in fall or spring as a weed-suppressing mulch (*see right*) and general soil improver. It is unsuitable for use as a substitute for potting mix in containers, as it is full of microbes—potting mix is sterilized.

Improving heavy soil It's easy to tell if your soil is heavy. If it sticks to your boots when wet, puddles when it's raining, cracks in dry weather, and possibly has a telltale film of green algae on the surface, it has a high clay content that prevents water from draining quickly. A simple solution is to dig in quantities of sand. You can buy this in bags at garden centers and DIY stores, but if you have a large area to deal with, it's more economical to have it delivered in bulk. Check that any product you buy is suitable for garden use. For heavy clay soils, dig in about one wheelbarrowful per square yard (meter).

Removing competing weeds Weeds are vigorous plants that suck up soil moisture and nutrients, to the detriment of all other plants. Controlling them is an important part of garden management. When digging over a site before planting, remove all traces of weeds, especially perennial weeds that have deep or spreading roots. Weed seedlings can usually be dealt with by hoeing. If there is a heavy weed infestation, it may be necessary to apply a weedkiller. For further advice on dealing with weeds, see Weed troubleshooter (*pp.112–13*).

Mulching A mulch is a top-dressing applied around plants directly onto the soil. All mulches help suppress weeds, but some bring other benefits as well. Garden compost, for example, looks unobtrusive. Earthworms drag the material down their tunnels, aerating the soil and opening up the structure. It also breaks down slowly and as it does so releases plant nutrients into the soil.

Sand is decorative but does not feed plants. Bark chips are an organic alternative; in time, they will break down and improve soil structure and fertility, but they will rob the soil of nitrogen in the process. To counteract this, fork in a fertilizer rich in nitrogen each spring.

Choosing plants

Many people find it difficult to know which plants to grow, especially when faced with a shady site. The following chapter helps you decide, with tips on identifying shade-lovers, and how to use and grow them in your garden. Before making your selection, first check how many hours of sunlight your garden receives, as many plants perform best when given a few hours of sun each day, while others will grow happily in areas that receive no direct sunlight at all.

Identifying shade-loving plants

It's a common mantra of gardening that you should restrict your choice of plants to those that are adapted to thrive in the conditions in your garden. But how do you tell which ones like shade?

Silver leaves are sun lovers With a few exceptions, plants with silver or gray leaves do not do well in shade. The leaves of such plants are actually green, but they have a coating, usually hairy, powdery, or waxy, that protects them against sun. The hotter it is, the more it develops. They are always at their most decorative in full sun.

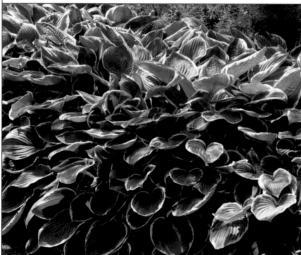

Perennials for shade Conversely, plants with very thin-textured leaves, such as many of the hostas and pulmonarias, can scorch in full sun and are always best in shade. Plants with variegated leaves need some sun to bring out the variegation—in deep shade, the leaves tend to revert to plain green. Site these where they will receive sun for just a few hours each day—but not harsh midday sun in summer—or where there will be a light leaf canopy above them that casts dappled shade. Perennials that are grown for their flowers, such as peonies, are often described in plant dictionaries and catalogs as suitable for sun or shade. They will flower more freely in sun, but the flowers will last longer and hold their color better in shade.

Fern effects Ferns are primitive plants that do not flower in the conventional sense. They are widespread in the wild, the majority preferring damp soil in shady sites. They are often found in woods or near water. Closely examined, the fronds show great diversity, many being crimped or crested or dwarfed. In the garden, ferns are excellent for bringing life to dark, dank corners, and always a good choice for planting near a shady water feature or in a rock garden. They are particularly attractive in dappled shade beneath deciduous trees. In a courtyard garden or on a shady patio, they can be grown successfully in containers, provided you keep them well watered. Evergreen species create outstanding features in a winter garden.

Shrubs for shade In the wild, shrubby plants often form the understory in forests, reveling in the cool spaces between taller-growing trees. Craning toward the light that filters down from above, they can themselves become treelike with age. The majority are tough, tolerant plants. Quite a few of the shrubs grown in gardens are actually woodlanders that thrive in shady conditions, and some, such as the *Sarcococca* shown here, can be used as ground cover. Shrubs with large leaves, such as hydrangeas, particularly appreciate the shelter provided by other, taller plants, while spring-flowering shrubs like rhododendrons and camellias offer weeks of spectacular blooms in lightly shaded situations. If you don't have acidic soil, grow the latter two plants in containers.

Light in winter The majority of bulbs that flower from late winter to spring are sun-lovers, but can be grown in areas that are predominantly shaded later on in the year. Use them to carpet the ground beneath deciduous trees, where they will complete their growth cycle while the tree is still leafless. By the time the emerging leaf canopy starts to blot out the sun—usually by late spring—the bulbs will have disappeared underground and become dormant. Choose for this purpose snowdrops (*Galanthus*), crocuses, anemones, and early-flowering daffodils (*Narcissus*). Most tulips flower too late to be used in this way.

Climbing to the sun Climbing plants are natural woodlanders. In the wild, they creep along the forest floor until they meet an appropriate host plant. This they scramble up with great vigor until they reach the leaf canopy, where they can spread out luxuriantly and turn their flowers to the sun. In gardens, climbers appreciate cool conditions around the roots and will then stretch toward the light. Plant them against shady walls, to climb into established trees, or to wander through a group of mixed shrubs. Where possible, train the stems horizontally to prevent all the flowers from appearing only at the top of the plant.

Trees and shrubs

Shrubs and trees are those plants with a permanent woody framework that provide a presence all year, offering leaf and flower color in the summer and structure in the winter.

Trees and shrubs for deep shade Evergreens with thick, glossy leaves do well in deep shade. They may not flower as freely as they would in more light, but most are valued as background plants to more flamboyant performers. As you get to know them, you learn to appreciate their understated charm—many have a handsome presence. Plants suitable for topiary, such as boxwood (*Buxus*), Portugal laurel (*Prunus lusitanica*), and yew (*Taxus*), make ideal container plants for a shady patio.

- *Aucuba japonica*
- *Buxus sempervirens*
- *Daphne laureola*
- *Ilex aquifolium*
- *Lonicera pileata*
- *Osmanthus decorus*
- *Prunus laurocerasus*
- *Sarcococca*
- *Taxus baccata*
- *Vinca*

Trees and shrubs for light and dappled shade Plants with soft leaves can suffer scorch in full sun and usually cannot tolerate a windy, exposed site. If your garden is sheltered and shady, you have solved both these problems. It's important that shrubs grown for their spring flowers, such as camellias, have adequate light, and these are best positioned where the sun can filter down, such as near deciduous trees or a trellis. Plants with variegated leaves need some sunlight to bring out the variegation.

- *Acer palmatum*
- *Berberis darwinii*
- *Camellia*
- *Dicksonia antarctica*
- *Hydrangea*
- *Paeonia*
- *Philadelphus*
- *Pieris japonica*
- *Rhododendron*
- *Skimmia japonica*

Growing tips for trees and shrubs

Staking Staking a tree helps develop a straight trunk and stops the plant from falling over, especially in a windy site. When planting, after you have positioned the tree in its planting hole, drive the stake in at an angle pointing into the prevailing wind and avoiding the rootball. Tie the tree to the stake with a rubber tree tie, which can be loosened as the trunk thickens. Remove the stake after three years.

Maintenance Most trees and shrubs need frequent and generous watering during the first spring and summer after planting, to help them settle in, and during extended dry periods a year or two after that. Once established, extra watering should not be necessary. Shrubs benefit from an annual dose of general fertilizer in spring.

Perennials

Like trees and shrubs, most perennials are long-lived, but they lack a woody framework. The majority die back in winter, reappearing the following spring.

Perennials for deep shade Some perennials thrive in shade, and will even flower, albeit discreetly. Soil in shade dries out less quickly than in sun (except under trees), and this suits certain plants. The majority of ferns do well in deep shade, provided the soil stays reasonably moist.

- *Brunnera macrophylla*
- *Convallaria majalis*
- *Dryopteris filix-mas*
- Plain-leaved hostas
- *Lamium maculatum*
- *Polygonatum* x *hybridum*

Perennials for light or dappled shade A huge number of perennials do well in a lightly shaded site. Even those that are often recommended for sun will tolerate shade, appreciating the cool soil, though they may not flower so freely. If in doubt, put the plant in and see what happens. Plants that don't perform well can be moved to a different spot in the spring or fall. Most perennials are very agreeable and don't mind this treatment.

- *Ajuga reptans*
- *Alchemilla mollis*
- *Bergenia*
- *Dicentra spectabilis*
- *Geranium macrorrhizum*
- *Helleborus*
- *Heuchera*
- *Kirengeshoma palmata*
- *Paeonia*
- *Tellima grandiflora*

Growing tips for perennials

Watering and fertilizing Keep perennials well-watered during the first growing season after planting, especially in periods of drought. Fork a general fertilizer into the soil around the plants each spring. A mulch of organic matter—garden compost or well-rotted farmyard manure—can be spread over the soil in spring or fall.

Maintenance Deadhead perennials after flowering. If they become congested after a few years, lift the plants in spring or fall and divide them into smaller pieces, either by pulling them apart with your hands, using two forks held back to back, or with a sharp garden knife. Replant the best parts and discard any old material.

Perennial performers Most shade-loving perennials are fast-growing, trouble-free plants. They soon fill out to produce a fine display every year, but die down in winter. Underplant with spring bulbs to fill this seasonal gap.

Bulbs

These perennials have a special mechanism that allows them to disappear underground and rest when conditions are unfavorable for growth, typically during freezing weather in winter and periods of drought in the summertime.

Spring bulbs Many bulbs flower in the early months of the year and are invaluable for providing bold sweeps of color before light levels reach their peak and when the garden is just beginning to emerge from its winter dormancy. Snowdrops (*Galanthus*) and winter aconites (*Eranthis*) are first, followed by the crocuses, daffodils (*Narcissus*), and bluebells (*Hyacinthoides*). Use them to carpet the ground under deciduous trees and shrubs, or in lawns. They are also ideal container plants. Crocuses are often sold in a mix of colors—white, yellow, and purple. If you find this too much, plant them, allow them to flower, then weed out your least favorite color.

- *Camassia leichtlinii*
- *Crocus chrysanthus* 'E. A. Bowles'
- *Crocus* 'Dutch Yellow'
- *Crocus tommasinianus*
- *Crocus vernus* subsp. *albiflorus* 'Pickwick'
- *Eranthis hyemalis*
- *Fritillaria meleagris*
- *Galanthus elwesii*
- *Galanthus nivalis*
- *Hyacinthoides non-scripta*
- *Muscari armeniacum*
- *Narcissus* 'Actaea'
- *Narcissus* 'Tête-à-tête'

Bluebells create a romantic sea of blue in early spring.

Robust daffodils and fritillaries do well in grass.

Bulbs for summer color Certain lilies (*Lilium*) are woodlanders that appreciate cool conditions, especially around the base of the plant. Elegant and often deliciously scented, they are aristocrats of the garden. With a few exceptions, most of the other summer bulbs need full sun.

- *Colchicum speciosum*
- *Crocosmia* 'Lucifer'
- *Lilium* Bellingham Group
- *Lilium henryi*
- *Lilium lancifolium*
- *Lilium martagon*
- *Lilium medeoloides* (right)
- *Lilium pardalinum*
- *Lilium pyrenaicum*
- *Lilium speciosum*

Planting and aftercare

Most bulbs are best planted as bare bulbs when fully dormant—plant spring-flowering ones in fall, and fall-flowering ones in late summer. Lily bulbs are usually planted in spring. Nearly all bulbs must have good drainage, so if your soil is on the heavy side, work in plenty of sand beforehand.

Plant them to twice the depth of the bulb, lilies even deeper—they like to be as deep as three times the depth of the bulb. Deadhead after flowering and feed with a general fertilizer to help build up the bulb for good flowering the following year. If you need to move bulbs, dig them up after flowering while they are still in growth.

To naturalize in a lawn, scatter dormant bulbs randomly and plant where they land.

Snowdrops are best planted while they are in full growth, just after flowering.

If clumps of bulbs become congested, dig them up after flowering and divide them.

Climbers

Adapted to varying degrees of shade, climbers are plants that lift your gaze skyward. Use them to embellish screens or walls, or to grow up and over arbors and arches.

Shady bowers Not many climbers do well in deep shade, but variegated ivy, used here to make an evergreen canopy over a garden seat, will cope with low light levels, and makes a refreshingly cool place to sit in the summer.

Climbers for light shade

Almost all climbers do well in partial shade, reveling in the cool conditions at their roots and stretching toward the light with great vigor. Climbers grown primarily for their flowers may not flower as freely as they would in full sun but will still provide a good display in light shade.

- *Akebia quinata*
- *Hydrangea anomala* subsp. *petiolaris*
- *Lonicera* x *tellmanniana*
- *Lonicera tragophylla*
- *Schizophragma integrifolium*
- *Trachelospermum jasminoides*
- *Wisteria sinensis* (right)

Supporting climbers

Climbers have evolved various strategies for attaching themselves to a support or host plant. Self-clingers have suckering pads or aerial roots for good adhesion. Others twine using their stems or modified leaf stalks or tendrils. Thorns act like sharp claws, clinging to rough bark. Most climbers need some training for optimum performance.

Self-clingers Ivies are evergreen climbers with aerial roots that enable them to cling to their support. On planting, tie stems to canes angled toward the support. Remove them once a good grip has been achieved.

Wrap-around climbers To persuade a twining leaf stalk or tendril climber to ascend an upright post, screw in vine eyes at regular intervals and stretch wires between them. Train stems onto the wires as they grow.

Tying in and training Most climbers will not attach themselves to a trellis without some help. Tie in stems as they grow, coaxing them as near the horizontal as you can in order to achieve good coverage.

Clematis

Sometimes called the "queen of climbers," clematis earn their place in gardens for their spectacular flowers in shades of white, pink, red, blue, and purple.

Upwardly mobile By carefully choosing from among the hundreds of varieties, it's possible to have a clematis in flower virtually every week from late winter to fall, with a peak in summer.

Species to grow into trees, and over arbors and buildings Many of the species clematis—and their hybrids—are plants of great vigor that flower prolifically. They do a terrific job of disguising ugly walls and outbuildings, though the cover is not permanent, most losing their leaves in fall. Many are also sensational when grown to fill out the branches of an existing tree, but you need to be sure that the host plant is well established and can bear the weight of the clematis.

- *Clematis flammula*
- *Clematis montana*
- *Clematis orientalis*
- *Clematis* 'Paul Farges'
- *Clematis rehderiana*
- *Clematis tangutica* (*right*)

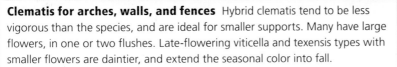

Clematis for arches, walls, and fences Hybrid clematis tend to be less vigorous than the species, and are ideal for smaller supports. Many have large flowers, in one or two flushes. Late-flowering viticella and texensis types with smaller flowers are daintier, and extend the seasonal color into fall.

- *Clematis* 'Beauty of Worcester'
- *Clematis* 'Fireworks'
- *Clematis* 'Hagley Hybrid'
- *Clematis* 'Huldine'
- *Clematis* 'Jackmanii'
- *Clematis* 'Margaret Hunt' (*above*)

Compact hybrids Some modern hybrids make compact plants, ideal for planting in patio containers and large hanging baskets.

- *Clematis* 'Burma Star'
- *Clematis* 'Silver Moon' (*above right*)
- *Clematis* 'Sunset' (*above left*)

Annuals and biennials

Annuals and biennials are short-lived plants with one season of glory only—but when that season arrives, their flowers seem to go on forever.

Plugging gaps in borders This border concentrates on foxgloves (*Digitalis*), which thrive very happily in shade. There is a wide variety of forms in a range of colors—white, pink, purple, and soft apricot yellow—all of which are easily raised from seed. Drop the young plants into any gaps in your borders in fall or spring. Foxgloves are biennials, and will flower the summer after planting.

Brightening up gloomy patios

Many of the shorter-growing annuals and biennials can be grown in containers and used to brighten a shady area. Summer containers can also be placed in borders to liven up a planting whose main season of interest has passed, or is yet to come. To get your plants growing quickly, place the container in sun initially, then move it into light shade as the buds start to show color. The display will then continue for many weeks, even longer with due care. Feed with a potash fertilizer to encourage the plants to flower to their maximum potential, and remember to snip off faded flowers to prolong the display. Plants in pots need watering less frequently than those in sun, but check them every day or two in summer.

- *Begonia*
- *Digitalis purpurea*
- *Impatiens*
- *Lobelia erinus*
- *Lunaria annua*
- *Myosotis*
- *Nemesia*
- *Nicotiana x sanderae*
- *Nicotiana sylvestris*
- *Pelargonium*
- *Primula*
- *Torenia fourieri*
- *Tropaeolum majus*
- *Viola* (right)

Growing tips for annuals

Annuals from seed While you can buy bedding plants from garden centers throughout spring and summer, it's easy and much cheaper to raise your own from seed from early spring onward. Fill pots, trays, or modules with multipurpose or seed-starting mix, water well, and allow to drain. Sow the seed thinly and cover with sifted potting mix to the depth recommended on the seed packet. Remember that most small seeds need light to germinate. Hardy annuals can be placed outdoors in a sheltered spot. Half-hardy annuals usually need warmth to get them going. Depending on the light requirement of the seed, a windowsill or warm cupboard can provide the appropriate temperature—or delay sowing until late spring.

When the seedlings are large enough to handle, pot them on individually or well spaced out in trays. Keep the seedlings well watered and apply a liquid fertilizer to encourage strong growth. Plant them out when large enough and, if growing tender types, after the last frost in late spring or early summer. Many hardy annuals can also be sown *in situ* where they are to flower.

Roses for shade

After centuries of extensive breeding, rose genes all are mixed up. Several varieties have inherited a tolerance for shade from some woodland ancestor—though none does well in deep shade.

Ramblers Even experienced gardeners are confused as to the distinction between ramblers and climbing roses. The demarcation line is actually rather blurred, but as a general rule, ramblers are vigorous plants with usually thorny, arching canes. Flowers, often small but in generous clusters, are carried in a single, breathtaking flush in early summer. Formal training against a wall or screen is possible, though many varieties consequently succumb to mildew late in the season. They're spectacular when allowed to romp unchecked through a tree.

- *Rosa* 'Albéric Barbier'
- *Rosa* 'Crimson Shower'
- *Rosa* 'Mme Plantier'
- *Rosa* 'Rambling Rector'
- *Rosa* 'Seagull' (*right*)
- *Rosa* 'Veilchenblau' (*below*)
- *Rosa* 'Wedding Day'

Climbers These roses usually flower in two flushes, or over a long period. Some are as vigorous as ramblers, others more modest. Train them against a wall or fence or over an arbor. If you are short of space, try a miniature.

- *Rosa* 'Danse du Feu'
- *Rosa* 'Golden Showers'
- *Rosa* 'Laura Ford' (min.)
- *Rosa* 'Maigold' (*below*)
- *Rosa* 'Mme Alfred Carrière'
- *Rosa* 'Mermaid'
- *Rosa* 'New Dawn'

Shrub roses It's always worth trying some of the tougher shrub roses in shade, but be warned: some will stretch toward the light and start behaving like climbers. If so, give them support and encouragement.

- *Rosa* 'Agnes'
- *Rosa* 'Ballerina' (*below*)
- *Rosa* 'Blanche Double de Coubert'
- *Rosa* 'Félicité Perpétue' (*right*)
- *Rosa* 'Frühlingsmorgen'
- *Rosa* 'White Pet'

Seasonal planner

This guide will help you to choose plants that can provide interest in a shady garden throughout the year. Most of the plants recommended are described in more detail, with hints on cultivation, in the Plant guide (*see pp.122–153*).

Winter

This is a quiet time in the garden, but there are still plants that attract attention.

Evergreen trees and shrubs

All woody plants have a strong presence. Evergreens, which can be variegated, give life to the garden. Try: *Euonymus fortunei, Ilex crenata, Trachycarpus fortunei.*

Stems and bark

Some trees and shrubs are grown for the interesting form or color of their bare winter stems. They look best when lit up by winter sun, but most tolerate a shaded position in summer. Try: *Betula, Cornus, Salix.*

Winter flowers

A number of shade-loving plants flower at this time of year. Some are deliciously scented to attract pollinating insects. Most perennials are dormant underground. Try: *Crocus tommasinianus, Cyclamen, Helleborus, Sarcococca, Vinca, Viola.*

Spring

This is a fresh time in the garden, when plants are emerging from winter dormancy.

Colorful bulbs

Spring bulbs are among the most valuable plants in the garden. For blocks or sweeps of color, they are unrivaled. Try: *Anemone blanda, Camassia leichtlinii, Crocus, Hyacinthoides non-scripta, Narcissus.*

Shrubs and perennials

The majority of hardy shrubs flower during the first half of the year, and many do well in dappled shade. Herbaceous perennials are appearing from below ground. Try: *Bergenia, Camellia, Dicentra, Euphorbia amygdaloides, Geranium, Paeonia, Pieris, Rhododendron.*

Flowering climbers

Group 1 clematis flower in the spring. Toward the end of their season, other hardy climbers join them. Try: *Clematis alpina, C. macropetala, C. montana, Wisteria sinensis.*

Some evergreen shrubs flower in winter, such as this mahonia, whose yellow blooms are also sweetly scented.

Hellebores and daffodils bring welcome color to the late winter and early spring garden.

Summer

This is the peak of the flowering year, when the garden is awash with flowers and scent—even the shady parts.

Seasonal blooms

All of the annuals are in flower now, as well as some climbers, perennials, and bulbs. This is also the time of year when roses come into their own, some filling the garden with scent. Try: *Aconitum, Begonia, Clematis, Crocosmia, Digitalis, Hemerocallis, Hydrangea, Impatiens, Lilium, Lobelia, Nicotiana, Rosa.*

Cool foliage

Some perennials and other plants are grown for their leaves as much as their flowers, and these can be superb, providing weeks of interest and a good contrast to flowers. Try: *Darmera,* x *Fatshedera lizei, Hedera, Hosta, Lamium, Paeonia,* plus ferns, bamboos, and sedges.

Scented stars

Many summer flowers have the advantage of a delicious fragrance. The slightly damper air in a shady spot "holds" scent, so your sheltered retreat can become a perfumed haven. Try *Hemerocallis, Hesperis matronalis, Hosta, Jasminum, Nicotiana, Rosa.*

Fall

This is a variable and sometimes short season in the garden. Pleasures are fleeting but memorable. This is mainly a time for fruits, berries, and leaf color, but, if regularly deadheaded throughout the summer, annuals and some roses will keep flowering right through until the first frost.

Leaf color

Most plants grown for fall leaf color perform best in sun, but there are exceptions. Try: *Acer japonicum, A. palmatum, Hosta, Rodgersia.*

Fall flowers

Flowers at this time of year are rare and precious. A sheltered site is important if they are to perform at their best. Try: *Anemone japonica, Colchicum speciosum, Fuchsia, Kirengeshoma, Tricyrtis formosana.*

Brilliant berries

Berries not only bring welcome color to the garden but are also an important food source for birds. Try: *Actaea rubra, Berberis darwinii, Hypericum, Rosa rugosa, Viburnum davidii.*

Tobacco plants (*Nicotiana*) are annuals with scented flowers that prefer cool conditions in light shade.

Japanese maples (*Acer palmatum*) are among the most reliable of all shade-tolerant trees for fall leaf color.

Simple planting projects

The following chapter offers advice on planting shade-lovers in a range of situations and for different seasons. Use the simple sequences to plant a shady border, create a cool rock garden, or make a water feature. In addition, you can bring welcome color to a shady patio or courtyard with a variety of containers, and use hanging baskets and window boxes to decorate vertical surfaces and bring a new dimension to your designs.

Making a shady border

A mix of perennials and shrubs offers an ideal low-maintenance border. The rhododendron here provides spring interest (if you have acidic soil), as do the dicentras, ajugas, and geraniums.

Tip for success

After planting a shrub, firm the soil gently with the ball of your foot to remove any air pockets around the roots.

1 Dig over the site before planting, and remove all weeds. Fork in plenty of organic matter—leaf mold, garden compost, and/or well-rotted farmyard manure. Work in sand if the soil is heavy and drains poorly.

2 Sprinkle a general fertilizer over the soil to feed the plants throughout their first growing season. This will gradually break down, releasing nutrients to the plants. Fork this lightly into the soil.

3 Arrange the plants in their pots to create a good design. For immediate impact, plant them fairly close together. In time, when they need more room, lift and split the perennials in spring or fall. Shrubs should stay put.

4 Dig holes so that each plant will be at the same depth as it was in its original pot. To check this, put the plant in its hole and lay a cane across the top. Backfill with soil, and water in well. Continue to water throughout the summer.

Planting a clematis

Clematis love cool conditions and thrive when their roots are in shade. This variety contrasts with the shade-loving climbing hydrangea.

1 Prepare the ground well before planting (*see p.59*). Dig a large hole that will allow for deep planting to keep the roots cool, and add some well-rotted compost to the bottom. Mix some more compost with the excavated soil.

2 Before you remove the plant from its pot, place it at the base of the hole and check the planting depth with a cane. It is beneficial to bury clematis stems to a depth of 2–3 in (5–7 cm).

3 Slide the clematis from the container and gently loosen the roots to help the plant establish quickly. Place it in the planting hole and insert a thin cane, angled toward the host plant or other support. Gently backfill the hole.

4 Tie the main stem loosely to the cane, using garden twine or plastic-coated wire ties. Be careful—clematis stems are brittle and easily snapped. If you have not already done so, fork a general fertilizer around the plant's base.

Creating a shady rock garden

Several shade-loving plants appreciate the cool conditions and good drainage that rocks provide. Most of the suitable plants flower in late spring, so make this the main season of interest.

1 Dig over the site well, making sure you remove all traces of perennial weeds. If the drainage is poor, dig in some sand. Mound up the soil if the site does not already slope naturally.

2 Set rocks into the soil, larger ones to the base of the mound. One-third to a half of each rock should be buried. Tilt the rocks forward slightly so that rainwater drains off them and away into the soil.

3 Arrange the plants in the gaps among the stones. A mix of ground-cover types, such as the periwinkle shown here, spring bulbs, small perennials such as ferns and hostas, ivies, and dwarf conifers works well.

4 Slide the plants from their containers and plant them in their allotted places. You may need to adjust the placement of some of the stones at this stage. Water the plants well until they are established.

Making a small water feature

While a true wildlife pond needs to be in sun to succeed, you can still enjoy water in a confined, shady spot on the patio near the house or in a courtyard garden.

1 Fix wooden battens painted with a preservative to the wall with long screws. These act as a mount for the trellis, which will conceal the water pipe. Be sure the battens are vertical so that the trellis panel attaches easily.

2 You can use a trellis panel just as it is, but painting it with a colorful preservative allows you to achieve a good link with other elements in the garden. Neutral or pale colors are the most sympathetic for a shady area.

3 Screw the trellis to the battens and then attach the mask: most can be hung on a long screw attached to the wall behind the trellis. Masks are usually made of stone, but you may also find fiberglass or resin alternatives.

4 If the pipe that fits the pump is a different gauge from the mask's feeder pipe, attach a short length of a pipe of the appropriate diameter for the mask. Seal the seam with silicone sealant and leave it to dry.

Making a small water feature *continued*

5 Feed the pipe behind and through the trellis. It should fit snugly over the mask's pipe and be watertight. If it isn't, run a line of sealant around the seam. Place a watertight barrel or other suitable reservoir in front of the trellis.

6 Connect the other end of the pipe to the pump. The pump must be sufficiently powerful to force the water from the reservoir up through the mask. Place the pump on a brick at the bottom of the barrel.

7 If you want to add plants, use aquatic baskets and aquatic potting mix. Regular potting mix has too many nutrients, which encourage algae to grow. Alternatively, use garden soil that has not had manure or pesticides added to it.

8 Top the soil surface with a layer of sand or small stones. This is important because it prevents the soil from rising up in the container and floating away into the surrounding water.

Tip for success

9 Lower the plants into the water gradually, allowing the water to saturate the soil through the holes in the sides of the aquatic basket. Adjust the plants until attractively positioned and then turn on the pump.

To make sure the plants are planted to the correct depth, stand them on bricks placed at the bottom of the barrel.

Planting a permanent container

A shrub or small tree in a container provides interest over a long period and can be used as a self-effacing partner to more flamboyant seasonal plantings elsewhere in the garden.

Tip for success

A layer of grit between the crocks and compost helps prevent waterlogging. Too much moisture encourages fungi to multiply.

1 Place pieces of broken clay pot (crocks) in the base of the container to cover the drainage holes. For extra stability, you could use pebbles. If weight is an issue, try chunks of polystyrene used in packaging.

2 Start filling the container with potting mix. For a permanent plant, a soil-based mix gives the best results, though multipurpose types can also be used. Work in a little slow-release fertilizer.

3 Slide the plant from its container and check the planting depth. Make sure the top of the soil is about 1 in (2.5 cm) below the rim of the container to allow for watering. Gently tease out the plant roots with your fingers.

4 Backfill around the rootball with potting mix. Firm the plant in with your fingers, then water well. Keep the container well watered throughout spring and summer. A layer of sand on the soil surface will help keep it moist.

Planting a summer container

Summer is a time for flowers. In a restricted space, a few large containers make a wonderful display. Here, purple heliotropes are mixed with nemesia, busy Lizzies, and evergreen lamium.

1 Place crocks at the bottom of the container and begin to fill with potting mix. To cut down on watering later on, add some water-retaining gel crystals to the mix at the rate recommended by the manufacturer.

2 Bring the potting mix up to the appropriate level and position your plants. Once planted, make sure that the top of the soil is 1 in (2.5 cm) below the rim of the container to allow for watering.

3 Carefully remove the plants from their pots and position them so they fill the container. Fill any gaps between the rootballs by sprinkling more potting mix through your fingers, and then firming it down gently.

4 Water the container well. You will need to water it daily thereafter, possibly twice a day at the height of summer. Feed either with pelleted fertilizer pushed into the soil or with a high-potash liquid fertilizer.

Planting a hanging basket

A well-planted hanging basket brings color to even the shadiest part of the garden. Baskets are usually hung from brackets on house walls, but can also be suspended from tree branches.

1 Hanging baskets are available in a variety of sizes and styles. Whatever design you opt for, the easiest way to plant the basket is to place it over a bucket or large pot in order to stabilize it.

2 Line the basket with moss or an alternative, such as the coir-based product shown here. If your basket is ready lined, proceed to Step 4.

3 To retain the potting mix (and moisture), make an inner lining with black plastic. An old potting mix bag provides the ideal material and is easily cut to the appropriate size. Make a drainage hole in the bottom of it.

4 Add a layer of potting mix to the bottom of the basket. You can use a special hanging basket mix or a lightweight multipurpose mix based on peat or coir. Soil-based mixes are too heavy for baskets.

Planting a hanging basket *continued*

5 To reduce the weight of the filled basket, stir in handfuls of perlite or vermiculite, as you fill it. At this stage, you can also add water-retaining gel crystals and a slow-release fertilizer to promote flowering.

6 Cut slits in the sides of the plastic with a sharp knife and start planting. Push the plants' rootballs carefully through the slits, and firm the soil over them. Here, busy Lizzies (*Impatiens*) and small ivies (*Hedera*) are used.

7 Continue filling the basket, planting the sides as you go. Once you have sufficient depth of potting mix, put in the accent plant at the top. A shade-loving fuchsia with trailing stems makes an ideal choice.

8 Fill any remaining gaps in the sides with more plants. For maximum impact, squeeze in as many plants as you can. As long as you continue to water and fertilize through the growing season, they will thrive.

9 Water the finished basket well. You will need to water it daily thereafter, possibly twice a day in the height of summer, but the plants will quickly grow and reward you for your efforts.

Planting a window box

You can bring color to a window sill that receives little or no direct light with a well-planted window box. This one has been planned for summer interest with colors that glow in darker corners.

1 If necessary, make holes in the base of the container for drainage and cover with a light layer of crocks or small stones. Add a layer of potting mix. You can also add water-retaining gel and slow-release fertilizer at this stage.

2 Slide the plants from their containers and set them on the soil surface. Make sure the top of the potting mix is 1 in (2.5 cm) below the rim of the box to allow for watering.

3 Fill around the plants with more potting mix. Put the box in position, then water well. Continue to water frequently throughout the summer while the plants are in full growth. Deadhead faded blooms to prolong flowering.

Planting lily bulbs in a pot

These lilies flower in sun, so keep them in a sunny site until the buds start to open, then move into shade to prolong their life. When in full growth, water lilies well so the buds develop fully.

1 In spring, buy fresh lily bulbs and select a large pot—most lilies need to be planted deep, at least 6–8 in (15–20 cm) below the soil surface. Line the base with crocks or stones and cover with a layer of potting mix.

2 Like most bulbs, lilies appreciate good drainage, so then add a layer of sand to a depth of about 1 in (2.5 cm) before planting them. Be careful not to buy limestone sand because some lilies are lime-hating.

3 Set the bulbs, which are composed of scales, on the sand. Put them on their sides to prevent water from filling the gaps between the scales, which could cause the bulbs to rot. Planting them like this doesn't affect flowering.

4 Continue filling the pot with potting mix, preferably blended with sand or perlite/vermiculite to improve drainage. Fill to about 1 in (2.5 cm) below the rim of the container to allow for watering. Top with a layer of sand.

Plug plants for a shady spot

While most annuals are easy to raise
from seed, begonias and busy Lizzies
(*Impatiens*) are more troublesome,
requiring conditions that are difficult to
replicate. Plug plants are the way to go.

1 Plug plants are well-developed seedlings that are sold in modules in the spring, and are much cheaper than fully grown plants. Look for them in garden centers, or buy them by mail order from a plant catalog.

2 Have some larger modules and potting mix ready for growing on the plantlets. After watering them well, gently ease the plantlets from their existing modules with a dibber or the end of a pencil.

3 Fill the larger modules with potting mix. Make a hole in the center of each module with your finger or a dibber and insert one of the plantlets. Be careful not to compact the soil around the plants.

4 Water the plants well, using a fine spray. Keep them in a sheltered, shady, frost-free spot. When the roots fill the cells, the plants can be put in their final positions after the last frost, either in the ground or in containers.

Plant combinations

Having identified the plants that will thrive in your garden, the next step is to devise ways of combining them to create exciting, seasonal displays. The following pages showcase a range of beautiful, easy-to-achieve planting recipes—the symbols below are used to indicate the conditions the plants prefer.

Key to plant symbols

Soil preference

◊	Well-drained soil
◗	Moist soil
●	Wet soil

Preference for partial or full shade

◐	Partial or dappled shade
●	Full shade

Hardiness ratings

✳✳✳	Fully hardy plants
✳✳	Plants that survive outside in mild regions or sheltered sites
✳	Plants that need protection from frost over winter
❅	Tender plants that do not tolerate any degree of frost

Spring mix

The main plant here is the Lenten rose (*Helleborus orientalis*), a handsome evergreen perennial with flowers in a range of colors—white, cream, soft red, and purple—and often dramatically spotted. The heuchera at its feet, which will flower later, has metallic, chocolate-purple leaves. Narcissi, flashing yellow in the background, do well in a site that will be heavily shaded in summer. The pansies and primulas are best treated as bedding plants, so you can vary the color scheme annually.

Border basics

Size 3 x 3 ft (1 x 1 m); to fill a larger space, increase the number of plants

Suits Informal shady border

Soil Fertile, not waterlogged

Site Cool, dappled shade

Shopping list

- 3 x *Helleborus orientalis*
- 5 x *Narcissus* 'February Gold'
- 3 x *Viola* 'Yellow Frost'
- 3 x *Primula vulgaris*
- 2 x *Heuchera* 'Amethyst Myst'

Planting and aftercare

Dig over the site, removing stones and weeds. Work in organic matter and/or a handful of slow-release fertilizer. If the soil is heavy, improve drainage by forking in a pail of sand.

The perennials are best planted in early spring. Dormant bulbs can be dropped in in fall, but it's also possible to buy them in containers ready for planting just as they are about to come into flower. Fill in any gaps with the bedding pansies and primulas, which are usually sold in small pots or polystyrene modules.

Keep new plantings well watered to help them establish—especially important if a nearby wall, fence, or large plant is creating a rain shadow. Deadhead all the plants as the flowers fade.

Helleborus orientalis
❋❋❋ ◊ ☀

Narcissus 'February Gold'
❋❋❋ ◊ ◊ ☀

Viola 'Yellow Frost'
❋❋❋ ◊ ☀

Primula vulgaris
❋❋❋ ◊ ☀

Heuchera 'Amethyst Myst'
❋❋❋ ◊ ◊ ☀

Summer pastel border

Most summer-flowering perennials are sun worshipers, but it's still possible to create interest in a shady spot if you accept that the result is likely to be subtle and soothing, rather than a brazen riot of vibrant color. Here, cool blues, soft pinks, and mauves make a harmonious blend with a pulmonaria, chosen for its mottled foliage, which gleams like old silver in the shadows. All these plants make excellent ground cover.

Border basics

Size 8 x 8 ft (2 x 2 m)

Suits Informal raised beds and borders

Soil Any well-drained

Site Light, dappled shade

Shopping list

- 3 x *Campanula poscharskyana*
- 3 x *Geranium* 'Blogold'
- 3 x *Phuopsis stylosa*
- 3 x *Pulmonaria* 'Diana Clare'

Planting and aftercare

It's best to make a border in spring or fall, but perennials can also be planted in early summer if the soil is moist and workable. The plants used here do not need rich soil, but if drainage is poor, dig in sand to improve the structure of the soil.

Depending on the size of the area, plant in groups of three or five, allowing gaps for the plants to spread. The campanula and *Phuopsis* are trailers that can be planted right at the edge of the bed and allowed to cascade down. If you have a dry stone wall, as shown here, you can fill some of the gaps with sandy soil and then push in small campanulas.

Keep the plants well watered until established. After a few years, if the plants outgrow their space, lift and divide them in the spring or fall.

Campanula poscharskyana
❀❀❀ ◊ ☀ ☀

Geranium 'Blue Sunrise'
❀❀❀ ◊ ◊ ☀ ☀

Phuopsis stylosa
❀❀❀ ◊ ◊ ☀ ☀

Pulmonaria 'Diana Clare'
❀❀❀ ◊ ☀ ☀

Fiery winter border

A surprising number of plants will provide interest in winter, and leaves, stems, and berries can be as attractive and eye-catching as flowers. Here, pollarded willows (*Salix*) lift the eye above a carpet of epimediums and snowdrops at their feet. Coppiced dogwoods (*Cornus*) create a screen of coral red stems. Epimediums are spring-flowering perennials with leaves that show bronze coloring when touched by frost. Hybrid snowdrops have larger flowers than the ordinary kinds.

Border basics

Size 10 x 10 ft (3 x 3 m)

Suits Medium-sized informal garden

Soil Moist but well-drained

Site Partially shaded, open area

Shopping list

- 5 x *Epimedium x perralchicum*
- 2 x *Salix alba* var. *vitellina* 'Britzensis'
- 3 x *Cornus alba* 'Sibirica'
- 30 x *Galanthus* 'S. Arnott'

Planting and aftercare

Prepare the site before planting. Plant the dogwood and willows first, forking plenty of organic matter into the excavated soil. Add the epimediums in spring or fall, allowing sufficient space between individual plants to accommodate their spread. Plant snowdrops in full growth in early spring.

To pollard a willow, allow it to develop a single trunk to the desired height, then cut back all the stems in late winter to form the head. Prune back the new growth every one or two years at the same time of year. To coppice dogwood, cut back all the stems to just above the ground every year in late winter. Clip over the epimedium foliage at the same time to expose the developing flowers. Dig up and divide the snowdrops after flowering if they become congested.

Epimedium
❋❋❋ ◐ ◇ ☀

Salix alba var. vitellina 'Britzensis'
❋❋❋ ◐ ◇ ☀

Cornus alba 'Sibirica'
❋❋❋ ◇ ◐ ☀

Galanthus 'S. Arnott'
❋❋❋ ◐ ◇ ☀

Japanese-style garden

Some shade-loving plants are of Japanese origin and can be combined to create a planting of Zen-like calm. The Japanese maple (*Acer palmatum*) to the back gives height, casting shade over the hostas and other perennials that like their toes in the cool soil between the rocks. Depending on the amount of light that filters down, choose plain-leaved or colored leaf/variegated perennials.

Border basics

Size 10 x 10 ft (*3 x 3 m*)

Suits Enclosed garden

Soil Reliably moist but not waterlogged

Site Semi- to deep shade

Shopping list

- 1 x *Acer palmatum* or *A. japonicum* cultivar
- 2 x *Hosta tokudama* f. *flavocirinalis*
- 1 x *Hosta sieboldiana*
- 3 x *Heucherella*
- 3 x *Hakonechloa macra*
- 3 x *Lysimachia nummularia* 'Aurea'

Planting and aftercare

The major purchase here is the tree. There are hundreds of types of Japanese maples: some make spreading mounds, others are taller and more airy, so choose one that suits the scale of your garden.

Plant in spring or fall, when the ground is workable. Fork in plenty of organic matter a few weeks before planting. Then dig a large hole for the tree and check that it will be slightly above the soil surface when planted. Stake the tree to prevent damage by wind. Position the rocks, and plant the perennials, ensuring that the variegated hostas and other plants that need some sun are sited beyond the tree canopy. Lay a bark or gravel mulch to keep the soil moist. Keep plants well watered during their first season. Paint the rocks with yogurt to encourage mosses.

Acer palmatum
❄❄❄ ◐ ◊ ☼

Hosta tokudama f. flavocirinalis
❄❄❄ ◐ ◊ ☼

Hosta sieboldiana
❄❄❄ ◐ ◊ ◐ ☼

Heucherella
❄❄❄ ◐ ◊ ◐ ☼

Hakonechloa macra
❄❄❄ ◐ ◊ ☼

Lysimachia nummularia 'Aurea'
❄❄❄ ◐ ◊ ☼

Planting for damp soil

One of the advantages of shade is that soil dries out more slowly than it does in sun. This suits many plants, which can grow lushly in a short space of time since they have a constant supply of water. This border of moisture-loving plants will provide color in late spring. So-called bog primulas are streamside plants that flower well in dappled shade, while hostas develop their lushest leaves when growing in permanently moist soil. In summer, the variegated hosta foliage will come into its own amid what will then be a predominantly green planting.

Border basics

Size 10 x 10 ft (3 x 3 m)

Suits Streamside or bog garden

Soil Heavy, moisture-retentive

Site Dappled shade

Shopping list

- 1 x *Viburnum plicatum* f. *tomentosum* 'Mariesii'
- 3–5 x *Primula japonica*
- 1 x *Hosta* 'Francee'
- 3–5 x *Digitalis purpurea* 'Alba'

Planting and aftercare

Make the border at any time between spring and fall when the soil is workable and neither too dry nor waterlogged. Dig in some well-rotted manure or garden compost, and remove all weeds. If the soil is heavy clay, dig in sand to improve drainage. Most damp soils are naturally high in nutrients, so you shouldn't need to add extra fertilizer.

Put the plants in their allotted positions. It's usual to place taller ones, such as the foxgloves (*Digitalis*), toward the rear, but you need not be too slavish about this. After the primula and foxglove flowers have faded, cut down the stems to the base. If congested, divide primulas after flowering and the other perennials in fall or the following spring.

Viburnum plicatum f. *tomentosum* 'Mariesii' ❄❄❄ ◐ ○ ☀

Primula japonica ❄❄❄ ◐ ○ ☀

Digitalis purpurea 'Alba' ❄❄❄ ◐ ○ ☀

Hosta 'Francee' ❄❄❄ ◐ ○ ☀

Alternative plant idea

Primula beesiana ❄❄❄ ◐ ○ ☀

Ivy league

Ivy (*Hedera*) is the natural choice for a very shady area, and if your heart is sinking at the prospect, think again. A visit to a specialty ivy nursery or a flip through a catalog—many of which are browsable online—will soon reveal the wide range of leaf shape and color available within this valuable, and undervalued, genus. Use them as ground cover, to clothe ugly walls, fences, or outbuildings, or as trailers in containers, hanging baskets, and window boxes. Here, a collection of ivies is used to dress a shady area beneath trees.

Border basics

Size 3 x 6 ft (1 x 2 m)

Suits Patio or courtyard garden

Soil Any well-drained, preferably alkaline

Site Dappled to deep shade

Shopping list

- 1 x *Hedera helix* 'Harald'
- 1 x *Hedera cristata*
- 1 x *Hedera helix* 'Little Diamond'
- 1 x *Hedera helix* 'Goldchild'

Planting and aftercare

Prepare the ground well prior to planting and dig in organic matter. If the drainage is poor, also dig in some sand. If you want the ivies to provide ground cover, after planting pin the stems to the soil with short lengths of bent wire—they will root where they touch the ground. Ivies do well in containers, the less vigorous types being most suitable. Here, an ivy is planted in a small plastic pot, which sits in the neck of the decorative jar. Any potting mix is suitable, but add a general slow-release fertilizer when planting and every spring. Ivies in the ground don't need fertilizer. Water frequently the first season after planting, and water the potted plant during dry periods. Once established, cut back the ivies as necessary in spring. You can clip over the plants again in midsummer.

Hedera helix 'Harald'
❀❀❀ ◐ ◇ ☀ ☀

Hedera cristata
❀❀❀ ◐ ◇ ☀

Hedera helix 'Little Diamond'
❀❀❀ ◐ ◇ ☀ ☀

Hedera helix 'Goldchild'
❀❀❀ ◐ ◇ ☀ ☀

Winter into spring container

To bring some color to the garden during that seemingly never-ending period at the end of winter, plant a container with a range of shrubs, bulbs, and annuals that provide interest at exactly this time. The *Pieris* used here was chosen for its brilliant young leaves. Buy polyanthus and dwarf daffodils when the buds are showing color—they will flower for several weeks.

Container basics

Size 2-ft- (60-cm-) diameter barrel

Suits Patio or courtyard garden

Soil Ericaceous potting mix

Site Light dappled shade

Shopping list

- 1 x *Vinca minor* 'Argenteovariegata'
- 4 x *Narcissus* 'Tête-à-tête'
- 1 x *Pieris* 'Flaming Silver'
- 3 x *Primula vulgaris* (polyanthus)

Planting and aftercare

In late winter, plant your container. Place crocks over the drainage holes at the base and begin to fill with potting mix. An ericaceous type is needed for the acid-loving pieris. If using another, non-ericaceous shrub, a soil-based or multi-purpose mix will be fine. Plant the shrub first, allowing a gap of up to 1 in (2.5 cm) between the top of the soil and the container's rim for watering. Position the smaller plants around the edge and fill in any gaps with more potting mix. Water the container well.

Deadhead the daffodils and polyanthus as the flowers fade. Remove the bulbs after flowering and either discard them or plant them out in the garden to flower the following year. Discard the polyanthus after flowering—use new plants next year. Fork in a general fertilizer in early spring and the *Vinca* and *Pieris* will rapidly grow to fill the container or can be planted out.

Vinca minor 'Argenteovariegata'
❋❋❋ ◗ ◊ ☀

Narcissus 'Tête-à-tête'
❋❋❋ ◗ ◊ ☀

Pieris 'Flaming Silver'
❋❋❋ ◗ ◊ ☀

Primula vulgaris (polyanthus)
❋❋❋ ◗ ◊ ☀

Shades of green

Hostas are surely the most versatile shade-lovers. Some are miniatures, ideal for a rock garden, while large-leaved varieties make sumptuous ground cover. Leaf shape varies, from broad and almost rounded to thin and pointed, and colors range from a luscious greenish yellow to a blackish dark green. Many desirable forms have thick, wax-coated leaves with a bluish cast. White, cream, or yellow markings can edge the leaves, or appear as bold central splashes.

Border basics

Suits Patio or courtyard

Soil Any well-drained soil or potting mix

Site Dappled to deep shade

Shopping list

- 1 x *Hosta* 'Ginko Craig'
- 1 x *Hosta* 'Francee'
- 1 x *Hosta* 'Wide Brim'
- 1 x *Hosta* 'Krossa Regal'
- 1 x *Hosta* 'August Moon'
- 1 x *Hosta fortunei* f. *aurea*

Planting and aftercare

You can create this hosta combination either in containers, as here, or in a shady bed. When planting in the ground, dig in organic matter, such as garden compost or well-rotted farmyard manure. To grow hostas in containers, use a soil-based potting mix. You can substitute a multipurpose mix, but will need to pay more attention to watering and feeding. Feed plants with an all-purpose fertilizer in spring.

Lift and divide congested plants in spring or fall. Very congested clumps can be cut into segments like a cake with a sharp knife. Control slugs and snails with slug pellets, or try copper bands around the rims of plant pots. Alternatively, water in pathogenic nematodes in spring to control slugs, and pick off snails by hand.

Hosta 'Ginko Craig'
❀❀❀ ◐◊ ☀

Hosta 'Francee'
❀❀❀ ◐◊◊ ☀

Hosta 'Wide Brim'
❀❀❀ ◐◊◊ ☀☀

Hosta 'Krossa Regal'
❀❀❀ ◐◊ ☀☀

Hosta 'August Moon'
❀❀❀ ◐◊◊ ☀

Hosta fortunei f. *aurea*
❀❀❀ ◐◊ ☀

Sunny colors in a shady pot

A small fuchsia with soft lime green foliage is the dominant plant in this combination. The daylily and creeping Jenny (*Lysimachia*) flower for a few weeks in summer, but the begonia and lobelia, as well as the fuchsia, will go on into early fall. Some houseplants grow well outdoors in the summer, and the spider plant here makes an excellent foliage plant for a container, its strappy leaves echoing those of the daylily.

Container basics

Container size 12 in (30 cm) or larger

Suits Patio or courtyard garden

Soil Soil-based potting mix

Site Light dappled shade

Shopping list

- 1 x *Fuchsia* 'Genii'
- 2 x *Begonia* x *tuberhybrida*
- 2 x *Hemerocallis* 'Stella d'Oro'
- 2 x *Chlorophytum comosum* 'Vittatum'
- 2 x *Lobelia erinus* 'Sapphire'
- 2 x *Lysimachia nummularia* 'Aurea'

Planting and aftercare

After the last frost, begin by covering the pot's drainage holes with crocks. Then start to fill with potting mix—either soil-based or a multipurpose one with added sand. Position the plants, with the trailers around the edges. Leave a gap of 1 in (2.5 cm) between the top of the soil and the rim of the pot for watering. Fill between the plants with potting mix and some slow-release fertilizer. Water the container well, and keep watering daily. Remove blooms as they fade to encourage further flowering. At the end of the season, discard the lobelia, and plant the perennials and fuchsia in the garden. Bring the spider plant indoors. Cut down the begonia stems, dry off the tubers, and store in a cool, dry, frost-free place over winter.

Fuchsia 'Genii'
✿✿✿✿ ◊◊ ☀

Begonia x *tuberhybrida*
✿✿ ◊ ☀

Hemerocallis 'Stella d'Oro'
✿✿✿ ◊◊ ☀

Chlorophytum comosum 'Vittatum'
✿ ◊◊ ☀

Lobelia erinus 'Sapphire'
✿✿✿ ◊ ☀

Lysimachia nummularia 'Aurea'
✿✿✿ ◊◊ ☀

Colorful shrub border

While all the shrubs in this border grow well in shade, some sun (and acidic soil) is needed for the rhododendron to flower successfully. The foliage shrubs—*Berberis* and *Euonymus*—also develop their best leaf color in partial shade, and continue to provide interest after the floral display has finished, along with the semievergreen fern. A planting like this takes three or more seasons to mature, but will continue giving pleasure with minimal maintenance for years after that.

Border basics

Size 10 x 10 ft (3 x 3 m); in a smaller area, substitute a dwarf rhododendron and trim back the other shrubs

Suits Woodland or informal garden

Soil Acidic, well drained

Site Light, dappled shade

Shopping list

- 1 x pink rhododendron
- 3–5 x *Berberis thunbergii* f. *atropurpurea*
- 3–5 x *Euonymus fortunei* 'Emerald 'n' Gold'
- 3–5 x *Dryopteris affinis*

Planting and aftercare

Make a shrub border in the spring or fall, but in cold areas, spring planting is best for evergreens, which tend to be slightly more vulnerable to frost damage. This gives them a whole growing season to settle in before their first winter. Dig over the site before planting, forking in plenty of organic matter. Work in sand if the ground is poorly drained. Plant the shrubs with space for them to grow, and apply a slow-release fertilizer. Keep well-watered, especially during dry spells in the summer. Deadhead the rhododendron after flowering, and apply a general fertilizer in spring and a mulch of garden compost in fall to help maintain soil fertility.

Pink rhododendron
❄❄❄ ◐ ◌ ☀

Berberis thunbergii f. *atropurpurea*
❄❄❄ ◌ ☼ ☀

Euonymus fortunei 'Emerald 'n' Gold' ❄❄❄ ◌ ☀

Dryopteris affinis
❄❄❄ ◐ ☀

Kitchen garden containers

Vegetables are normally grown in an open, sunny spot, but there are a few that will tolerate shade, particularly those with thin leaves that tend to flower and run to seed in hot conditions. The cut-and-come-again salad leaves shown here are particularly valuable. Just a few plants can provide fresh leaves for salads throughout summer. Mint and parsley also do well in shade. Apart from the mint, the only perennial, these plants are easily raised from seed.

Border basics

Size 3 x 3 ft (1 x 1 m) or larger

Suits Courtyard or patio

Soil Soil-based or multipurpose potting mix

Site Lightly shaded

Shopping list

- Lettuce 'Can Can'
- *Tropaeolum*, annual type
- Lettuce 'Lollo Rossa'
- Mixed leaves
- Mint
- Flat-leaf parsley

Sowing and aftercare

Sow seed from spring onward. Fill seed trays or small pots with potting mix, water well, and allow to drain. Sow seeds on the surface and cover with a light layer of potting mix. Place in a sheltered spot. Alternatively, sow seeds directly where they are to grow. When the seedlings are large enough to handle, pot them on into larger pots, if necessary. Keep them well-watered and you should be picking leaves within six to eight weeks. Make further sowings throughout spring and summer to ensure you have a ready supply of leaves.

Young nasturtium (*Tropaeolum*) leaves have a peppery taste and can be added to salads, as can the decorative and colorful summer flowers.

Lettuce 'Can Can'
❄ ◐ ◊ ☀

Tropaeolum, annual type
❄ ◐ ◊ ☀

Lettuce 'Lollo Rossa'
❄ ◐ ◊ ☀

Mixed leaves
❄ ◐ ◊ ☀

Mint
❄ ❄ ❄ ◐ ◊ ☀

Flat-leaf parsley
❄ ◐ ◊ ☀

Strawberry tower

Strawberries do best in a cool climate. Most of the hybrid forms need sun to ripen the large berries, but the species from which they have been bred—sometimes called alpine strawberries—are actually woodland plants that produce small, dark red fruits of incomparable flavor. A strawberry planter or tower is a tall pot with side pockets for planting. It won't provide a large enough crop for jam-making, but there should be enough for scattering over your breakfast cereal for quite a few weeks in the summer. Add a couple of shade-tolerant annuals, such as these begonias, for aesthetic appeal.

Container basics

Size Large strawberry pot

Suits Patio or courtyard

Soil Potting mix

Site Lightly shaded

Shopping list

- 5 x Alpine strawberry
- 1 x Angel wings begonia
- 3 x *Begonia* Cocktail Series

Planting and aftercare

Line the base of the tower with crocks or stones to cover the drainage holes, then start to fill with potting mix. When you reach the level of the lowest pockets, position the strawberries or other chosen plants in them and feed in potting mix around the rootballs. Continue filling the tower in the same way until all the pockets and the top are planted.

Keep the plants well watered during the summer. They must not be allowed to dry out while the fruits are swelling and ripening. Feed with a tomato fertilizer during spring and summer.

Continue to pick the fruits to encourage the plants to keep producing. Also deadhead the flowering plants to maintain the display.

Alpine strawberry flower
❄❄ 💧 ◌ ☀

Angel wings begonia
❄ 💧 ◌ ☀

Alpine strawberry in fruit
❄❄ 💧 ◌ ☀

Begonia Cocktail Series
❄ 💧 ◌ ☀

Caring for shady yards

The key to a pest- and disease-free garden is to be vigilant and to act quickly as soon as problems arise. Do this and your plants should thrive. It is also important to keep weeds at bay, and to maintain shady lawns to promote lush, healthy growth. In addition, remember that patios and hard surfaces will look neater and be less slippery if they are cleaned regularly. Follow the tips and advice in this chapter to keep your shady garden looking good throughout the year.

Watering and fertilizing

If your garden is to stay looking fresh and at its best, it will need some regular care, but with a little forethought and good time management, the tasks need not be onerous.

What and when to water All new plantings benefit from regular watering, especially during periods of drought when the soil dries out. Established plants, particularly trees and shrubs, usually do not need supplementary watering. Plants in pots need watering throughout spring and summer, and during long dry periods at other times.

Efficient watering Use a watering can to water individual plants, so that you can direct water over plant roots where it is needed. A "rose" on the can delivers the water as a spray, which is less likely to compact soil or wash it away from roots than a solid jet. A hose is useful for watering large areas, but can be wasteful. To water efficiently, direct the hose around the base of your plants rather than over the foliage, and make sure the ground is thoroughly soaked. It's best to water in the evening or early morning, when less water is lost through evaporation.

Drip hoses (*shown left*) are more efficient than spray types. These perforated rubber hoses are laid directly onto the soil around plants, with one end attached to the faucet. They deliver water slowly into the soil, and when disguised with a mulch offer a discreet method of watering.

Automatic systems Drip hoses can also be connected to an electronic automatic timer that releases the water at set times of the day. This makes it easier to water regularly at the appropriate times, and means that your garden will continue to be watered when you are away. During prolonged periods of drought, set your timer for longer or the amount of water delivered may be inadequate.

Drip irrigation systems are also available for plants in containers. These comprise one long tube, which you attach either to a garden hose, or to an automatic timer. You then attach smaller spur pipes with nozzles at one end to the main pipe, and insert these nozzles into the soil in your pots. These systems are a bit tricky to install but ensure that your pots are watered regularly and efficiently, and keep plants looking good throughout the season.

Choosing fertilizers Three major elements are needed for good plant growth. Nitrogen (N) promotes healthy leaf development, potassium (K) stimulates flower and fruit production and firms woody material, and phosphorus (P) encourages root growth. Other elements, known as trace elements, are necessary in much smaller quantities. General garden fertilizers contain the major elements in equal amounts, but you can also buy plant food that has a high nitrogen or potassium content, depending on the needs of the plant. For example, a lawn will require a nitrogen fertilizer, while potassium (potash) will help a summer bedding display. Some granular fertilizers are slow-release—they break down slowly in the soil and deliver nutrients to plants over several weeks. Liquid fertilizers provide an instant boost—apply them as a root drench or spray over topgrowth as a foliar fertilizer.

Berries are encouraged with applications of potassium.

Potassium promotes flower formation.

Nitrogen helps plants develop lush leaves.

Applying fertilizers Permanent plantings of shrubs and perennials need no more than an annual application of a general fertilizer in spring. Sprinkle the granules around the plants and lightly fork them in. A nitrogen-rich fertilizer can help get the plants going after their winter dormancy. Potassium-rich fertilizers are applied in spring to all plants grown primarily for their flowers. A further feeding in summer is beneficial to those plants that flower on through the season, such as roses, with an extra dose in late summer to firm the wood before winter. Don't use fertilizer in fall, as it promotes sappy growth, which is vulnerable to frost damage. Annuals are best fertilized in spring and summer with a potash root drench. Alternatively, add a slow-release fertilizer to the soil when planting, which will feed the plants for about six to eight weeks—after this time, you may need to top them off.

Add slow-release fertilizer to pots.   Fertilize beds annually.

Weed troubleshooter

Weeds are a problem in all gardens. They are best dealt with as quickly as possible, as they spread rapidly—either by seed or by sending out long runners underground—until they form dense mats that choke the plants that you have worked so hard to keep.

Hoeing A hoe is a useful tool that enables you to weed without bending down to ground level. However, it can be used only on annual weeds that are in the early stages of growth. Move the blade just beneath the soil surface to sever the topgrowth from the roots. On dry days, the weeds can be left where they are to wither and decay—on damp days there is a chance that they will re-root into the soil, so pick them up and compost them unless they have already set seed. For maximum efficiency, keep your hoe blade clean and sharp.

Hand weeding A very successful way of dealing with weeds, though labor-intensive, is to dig over the soil and take them out by hand. This is one of the best ways of removing perennial weeds that are deep-rooted or that produce mats of roots. When pulling out the roots, make sure you remove them in their entirety. If you leave behind any broken pieces of root or stem, they will produce more growth.

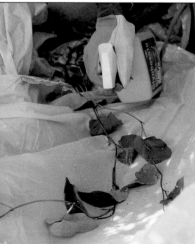

Using chemicals Weedkillers are useful on perennial weeds. Available as liquids or powders to be diluted, or ready-to-use sprays, most are applied to leaves when the weeds are in full growth in spring. Spray both surfaces for maximum effect—any that falls on the soil will be rendered inactive, but protect neighboring plants with a plastic sheet. Apply chemicals on a still day, when the product will not blow onto other plants. Dispose of any excess chemicals according to the manufacturer's instructions.

Dealing with common weeds

Dandelion This pernicious perennial spreads by seed, and has a long tap-root. Use a chemical spot weedkiller or dig out the taproot by hand.

Dock A perennial weed that disappears underground in winter. Apply a chemical weedkiller in spring or fall, or dig out by hand.

Ground elder This perennial weed spreads rapidly to form mats. Treat with a chemical weedkiller; several applications may be necessary.

Horsetail Horsetail is difficult to kill with most weedkillers. Covering with heavy-duty, light-excluding black plastic may keep it under control.

Stinging nettle The leaves of this perennial weed exude a skin irritant. Wear thick gloves to remove by hand, or control with a chemical weedkiller.

Lesser celandine This pretty weed thrives in damp soil. After treating with weedkiller, or digging it up, dig sand into the soil to improve drainage.

Bramble The stems of brambles root where they touch the ground. Cut to the ground in spring and apply a weedkiller when the leaves emerge.

Groundsel This annual weed seeds prolifically, spreading rapidly. Hoe out at the seedling stage or treat with a weedkiller.

Bindweed The roots of this climbing perennial are extensive, and make it difficult to dig out once established, so control with a chemical weedkiller.

Keeping pests at bay

Insects and other pests are a problem for all gardeners. Most are easily dealt with, especially if you grow a wide range of plants that attract pest predators to help control them for you.

The barrier method Physical barriers that pests are unwilling or unable to negotiate are an environmentally friendly method of control. Copper bands around the rims of containers filled with hostas and other vulnerable plants deter slugs and snails, or try crushed eggshells and cocoa shells spread around plants.

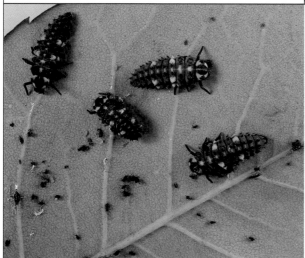

Know your friends A number of insects and other animals that themselves do no harm to plants prey on pests, and should be encouraged into the garden. Ladybugs and their larvae (*pictured left*) feed on greenflies and other aphids, as do the larvae of lacewings and hoverflies. The adults of the latter two can be encouraged to visit your garden by planting open-flowered plants.

Frogs and toads eat slugs and other pests, and will often appear unannounced if you have a pond. Remember that frogs and toads appreciate large stones, long grass, and other cool, shady places in which to shelter on hot days.

Controlling pests Many insect pests and their larvae can be picked off plants by hand and crushed if barrier methods haven't worked (*see above*). Pests are usually more easily controlled in small numbers, so check plants regularly to prevent infestations. In some instances, you may wish to use an insecticide, but remember that many, including some organic types, will kill friendly insect pest predators too. Contact insecticides kill pests directly; others are sprayed onto the plant and enter the pest's system as it feeds. Always wear gloves and protective goggles when spraying insecticides, and be sure to follow the manufacturer's instructions on use, storage, and disposal. Controls using pathogenic nematodes that prey on specific pests offer an organic alternative to chemicals.

Identifying common pests

Vine weevil larvae Adults are black beetles that lay eggs from late spring to early autumn. The larvae (*above*) eat roots and can kill plants, especially those in pots. Control grubs with a pathogenic nematode or thiacloprid drench in late summer.

Slugs and snails Molluscs love damp, shady areas and will chomp through hostas, seedlings, and the soft young growth of virtually any plant. Control them with slug pellets, copper bands, or apply a pathogenic nematode (effective on slugs only).

Lily beetles This bright red beetle and its lavae, which are orange-red grubs with black heads, feed on lilies and fritillaries. Check over the leaves of vulnerable plants regularly, and pick off and squash any beetles and grubs, or spray with imidacloprid.

Aphids Blackfly, greenfly, and other aphids suck the sap from a wide range of plants. Check plants regularly and squeeze small numbers between your fingers. Control severe infestations with imidacloprid or bifenthrin, or use organic sprays, such as pyrethrum or rotenone.

Capsid bugs These small green or yellowish-brown insects suck sap from buds and shoot tips. Their feeding damages developing leaves, causing them to tear into many small holes. Spray susceptible plants with bifenthrin from late spring onwards, when damage is first seen.

Solomon's seal sawfly larvae Black adult sawflies lay eggs in the leaf stalks of Soloman's seal. The greyish-white larvae can defoliate a plant in early summer but it will survive. To control, pick off larvae or spray with pyrethrum, rotenone, or bifenthrin when damage begins in late spring.

Controlling diseases

Plant diseases are caused by fungi, bacteria, and viruses. Fungal diseases are a particular problem in cool, shady sites because fungal spores require water to germinate, and moisture is slower to evaporate in the shade.

Keeping diseases at bay Good garden hygiene can help keep plants disease-free. Clear fallen leaves, which can harbor fungal spores. Prune shrubs to keep them growing strongly, and cut back diseased stems to healthy wood. Burn or bag the diseased material, rather than composting it. Also prune out congested stems to improve air flow—higher humidity encourages fungal growth.

Resist attack Choose plants that are adapted to your garden's soil conditions and light levels. Unhappy plants will be weak and susceptible to disease. To keep plants healthy, water and fertilize them sufficiently, but avoid overfertilizing, especially with nitrogen, as the sappy growth this encourages can be vulnerable to disease.

Chemical controls You can control many fungal diseases with fungicidal sprays. Certain bacterial diseases can also be controlled with chemicals. "Organic" products are based on naturally occurring materials. For optimum effect, spray upper and lower leaf surfaces. Viruses cannot be controlled with pesticides.

Identifying common diseases

Powdery mildew This disease causes a powdery coating on plants. It is associated with poor ventilation and dry roots. Cut off and destroy affected growth, prune congested stems, and apply an appropriate fungicide. Avoid overhead watering.

Coral spot This troublesome fungus affects woody plants, entering through wounds, often the result of careless pruning. Shoots die back and show coral red pustules of spores. Prune and burn or bag affected stems, sterilizing blades between cuts.

Downy mildew This fungal disease is a particular problem during cool, wet weather. Typically, leaves show brown spots, sometimes with a furry growth on the undersides. Cut off affected parts and spray plants with an appropriate fungicide, if available.

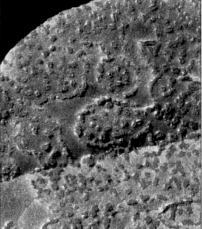

Sooty molds These molds do not attack plants directly but grow on the honeydew secreted by aphids and scale insects. Cut off badly affected growth or wash off any mold with water. Identify and control the pest causing the problem.

Leaf spot A number of fungi cause black spotting on leaves, and roses are particularly susceptible to this disease. Cut off and destroy affected growth and collect any fallen leaves. Spray with a fungicide and then boost growth with a liquid fertilizer.

Rusts Rusty red, brown, or yellow patches, caused by specific fungi, can appear on leaves, causing unsightly damage but seldom death. Cut off and destroy affected growth. Spray with an appropriate fungicide and choose rust-resistant plant species.

Caring for shady surfaces

Hard surfaces in shade present certain problems that occur less often in full sun. All benefit from attention once or twice a year if they are to stay clean and retain their good looks.

Patio dirt busters Hard surfaces in the shade tend to go green. Surface water evaporates less quickly so they stay damp for longer, allowing water-borne fungal spores, algae, lichens, and mosses to take a hold. Deal with any such growth promptly. Not only is it unsightly, but it can be dangerous, as it makes the surface very slippery when wet. Clean the patio with a sharp jet of water delivered from a pressure washer. Alternatively, use a patio cleaner that contains an algae and moss killer. In a small area, you could use a scrub brush.

Retouching paintwork

Painted walls may show signs of green algal growth. In the short term, this isn't disfiguring, but in time, the combined effects of wind and rain make the paint flake off to expose the brickwork below, which is less attractive. A wall will probably need repainting every three to five years, but you can touch it up annually to maintain a beautiful, clean backdrop for your borders or patio container displays.

Rub down the walls to remove flaking paint.

Repaint with a masonry paint of the desired color.

Protecting lumber All wood used outdoors has a limited life. As it is a natural material, it's subject to decay, though its durability can be improved with care and attention. Soft wood is much more likely to rot than hard wood, and the latter is consequently more expensive. You should also always check that the trees used to make hard wood products are from a renewable source, and not illegally logged from rainforests or other environmentally sensitive areas. Treat hardwood benches and tables with teak oil every other year or so. Fences and decks, usually made of soft wood, should be painted annually with a wood preservative. Wooden containers for planting can also be treated, but make sure that any paint, stain, or preservative you use is plant-friendly—some are toxic.

Cleaning stone and concrete Depending on the context, a certain amount of algal growth can add to the appeal of stone and concrete, though not when it is underfoot. Around a water feature, especially if you are looking for an authentic Venetian palazzo look, algae- and moss-clad stone has a definite charm. With a constant play of water, mosses will eventually appear anyway, but they can be encouraged with a wash of yogurt. In a more contemporary setting, you may prefer to retain a clean, sheer, light-reflecting surface. To keep stone and concrete clean, scrub it down regularly with bleach or a detergent to remove any green patches. For stubborn stains try a "wet and dry" abrasive pad (*left*), which is used to rub down scratches on car body paint.

Caring for terra-cotta pots Many gardeners prefer terra-cotta containers to plastic because the traditional material ages much more sympathetically. This porous material allows moisture and air to percolate through the sides. However, the water can cause ugly staining as mineral salts dissolved in it leave behind a whitish deposit on the pot after the moisture has evaporated. Clean with a wire brush dipped in detergent.

All terra cotta is vulnerable to frost damage to some degree. Do not water plants during very cold weather, as the water retained by the compost will expand as it freezes, cracking the terra cotta. For additional protection, wrap large containers in burlap or bubble plastic when hard frosts are forecast.

Lawn care for shady sites

Most of us put our lawns to heavy use, especially during the summer. Annual maintenance will keep grass looking good and fit for its purpose, and although a shady lawn has its own problems, they are easy to deal with.

Lawn weeds Common lawn weeds, including daisies and dandelions, can be dug up individually or by hand. A daisy or dandelion digger is a special tool that makes it easy to extract the deep roots, or use a knife to cut around the taproots. Alternatively, apply a lawn or spot weedkiller before the weeds flower.

Reseeding Bald patches often appear on lawns, especially if they have suffered heavy traffic. Repair them in spring or fall by lightly forking over the area and sprinkling with a grass seed mix recommended for shade. Water well to ensure good adhesion. Do not mow the area until the new grass is at least 2 in (5 cm) high.

Feeding All lawns benefit from fertilizing in spring. Use a special lawn fertilizer that is high in nitrogen to promote lush green growth. Some products also contain weedkillers, and seed to help thicken the existing grass. Lawn treatments containing iron make the grass appear healthier by darkening the green, but they don't fertilize.

Routine lawn care

Raking In the fall, rake the lawn to remove "thatch," a buildup of dead grass and debris that collects around grass stems, preventing water from draining freely. Poor drainage encourages moss, always a problem in shade. Then treat the lawn with a moss killer. After two weeks, rake off the dead moss, and aerate (*see right*).

Aerating After raking, drainage needs to be further improved to allow rainwater to penetrate down to the grass roots, reducing the risk of "puddling" on the surface. Drive in a fork at regular intervals all over the lawn, rocking it to create bore like holes in the ground. This also encourages the grass roots to grow.

Top dressing To reinvigorate a lawn after it has been raked and aerated, cover the whole area with a topdressing of equal parts lawn sand and finely sifted garden compost, leafmold, or topsoil, together with some grass seed. This procedure is best done using a shovel or spade on a dry day.

Brushing in Brush the mixture over the lawn with a stiff brush or twig broom to ensure that coverage is even and that the top-dressing fills the aeration holes. Avoid walking over the surface of the lawn for a week or so, if possible. You will find that the top-dressing will be rapidly absorbed into the lawn.

Plant guide

The following plants are ideal for shady areas, and will enliven sites in light, dappled, or deep shade, so whatever your garden conditions, there is something here to suit them. The symbols below are used in the guide to indicate the growing conditions the plants prefer.

Key to plant symbols

Soil preference

○	Well-drained soil
◐	Moist soil
●	Wet soil

Preference for partial or full shade

☀	Partial or dappled shade
☀	Full shade

Hardiness ratings

❋❋❋	Fully hardy plants
❋❋	Plants that survive outside in mild regions or sheltered sites
❋	Plants that need protection from frost over winter
❀	Tender plants that do not tolerate any degree of frost

Plant guide (Ac–An)

Acer palmatum *'Bloodgood'*

A beautiful Japanese maple, valued for its elegant, handlike, rich purple leaves that turn spectacular shades of orange and red in fall. In time, it grows into an evenly shaped dome. Some sun is needed if the purple is to be retained throughout summer.

H: 8 ft (2.5 m); **S**: 10 ft (3 m)
❄❄❄ ◊ ☀

Acer palmatum *'Butterfly'*

This cultivar is more upright than many other Japanese maples, and with its cream- and pink-margined leaves makes an ideal focal point. Some sun is needed to bring out its colors, as well as shelter from cold winds, essential while foliage unfurls.

H: 10 ft (3 m); **S**: 5 ft (1.5 m)
❄❄❄ ◊ ☀

Acer palmatum *'Sango-kaku'*

This maple is clothed in bright orange-yellow leaves that turn butter yellow in fall. Its coral red stems then become a feature. Site the tree to be lit up by the fall sun, making sure there is adequate shade in spring and summer to shield the foliage.

H: 20 ft (6 m); **S**: 15 ft (5 m)
❄❄❄ ◊ ☀

Aconitum *'Bressingham Spire'*

Aconites, or monkshoods, are distinctive but sinister-looking perennials with spires of hooded flowers. 'Bressingam Spire' produces its deep violet flowers from midsummer to early fall. The tall flower stems may need staking.

H: 36–40 in (90–100 cm); **S**: 12 in (30 cm) ❄❄❄ ◐ ☀

Actaea rubra

Red baneberry is grown less for its late spring white flowers than for the luscious red berries that succeed them in fall. Dying back in winter, it is excellent either in a shady border or in a woodland planting. The berries are poisonous.

H: 18 in (45 cm); **S**: 12 in (30 cm)
❄❄❄ ◐ ☀

Actaea simplex

This plant, formerly *Cimicifuga*, is a stalwart of the shade border, producing its wandlike spikes of white flowers on tall stems amid ferny foliage in late summer. It likes cool conditions with some shelter. The stems may need staking.

H: 4 ft (1.2 m); **S**: 24 in (60 cm)
❄❄❄ ◊ ☀

Ajuga reptans

A delightful ground cover perennial that rapidly spreads by runners to create mats of burnished foliage. In late spring, the plant is enlivened by spires of blue, pink, or white flowers. Some forms have colored leaves and need a little sun for the best effect.

H: 6 in (15 cm); **S**: 36 in (90 cm)
❄❄❄ ◐ ☼ ☀

Alchemilla mollis

Lady's mantle's modest presence belies its thuggish tendencies—it's a great colonizer. The felted leaves are appealing and the frothy lime green flowers blend with virtually all other plants. Cut back faded flowers to prevent them from seeding.

H: 24 in (60 cm); **S**: 30 in (75 cm)
❄❄❄ ◐ ☼

Anemone blanda

For a wash of blue beneath deciduous trees or among shrubs in early spring, this corm, with its daisy-like flowers, is unmatched. Pink and white forms, as well as mixtures, are also available. Soak dry corms for 24 hours before planting in fall.

H: 6 in (15 cm); **S**: 6 in (15 cm)
❄❄❄ ○ ☼

Anemone x hybrida

Japanese anemones are among the few hardy perennials that flower at the tail end of summer. The bowl-shaped flowers, white or in delicate shades of pink, are carried on strong but elegant stems. Breathtaking in the dappled shade under trees.

H: 4–5 ft (1.2–1.5 m); **S**: 24 in (60 cm)
❄❄❄ ◐ ☼

Anemone nemorosa

The wood anemone is a vigorous woodlander that spreads to create a low-growing carpet studded with white, daisylike flowers in late spring. 'Bracteata Pleniflora', shown here, has double flowers that are held above a ruff of green leaves.

H: 3–6 in (8–15 cm); **S**: 12 in (30 cm)
❄❄❄ ○ ☼

Anemonella thalictroides

A modest plant with attractive bluish-green leaves. The daisylike white or pale pink flowers, produced from spring to early summer, are cupped rather than opening flat. Slow to establish but worth persevering with, rue anemone is good in a rock garden.

H: 4 in (10 cm); **S**: 12 in (30 cm)
❄❄❄ ◐ ☼

Plant guide (Aq–Be)

Aquilegia vulgaris *var.* stellata *'Norah Barlow'*

This aquilegia is valued for its unusual coloring—soft pink, cream, and green. Use it in combination with other late-spring-flowering perennials or less formally in light woodland.

H: 36 in (90 cm); **S**: 18 in (45 cm)
❄❄❄ ◊ ☀

Arisaema candidissimum

A plant for connoisseurs, this needs to be seen in isolation so that it does not have to compete for attention. Its pink and white spathe emerges in summer, before the leaves. The whole plant dies back below ground in winter. It needs neutral to acidic soil.

H: 16 in (40 cm); **S**: 6 in (15 cm)
❄❄❄ ◊ ☀

Arum italicum *'Pictum'*

A plant for winter interest, this bulb pushes up its shiny, marbled leaves in winter. They die back again in late spring. Spikes of juicy-looking, but poisonous, berries are sometimes seen in fall. The leaves collapse after a hard frost but rapidly recover.

H: 12 in (30 cm); **S**: 6 in (15 cm)
❄❄❄ ◊ ☀

Aruncus dioicus

Goatsbeard is a stately perennial that produces loose cones of creamy white flowers from early summer. It is an adaptable plant that can be used in borders or light woodland, but is perhaps seen at its best near water. The flowers are good for cutting.

H: 4 ft (1.2 m); **S**: 18 in (45 cm)
❄❄❄ ◖ ☀

Aspidistra elatior *'Variegata'*

The cast-iron plant is usually grown as a houseplant, but is more or less hardy, so worth trying in a sheltered spot near the house. Alternatively, it may be incorporated in a summer bedding scheme or container and brought indoors in winter.

H: 24 in (60 cm); **S**: 24 in (60 cm)
❄❄ ◊ ☀ ☀

Asplenium scolopendrium

For year-round interest in a rock garden, the evergreen hart's-tongue fern has much to offer. Its shiny green fronds always look fresh, while possibly succumbing to rust in wet winters. Look for forms with crimped or irregularly toothed leaf margins.

H: 18–28 in (45–70 cm); **S**: 24 in (60 cm) ❄❄❄ ◊ ☀

Astilbe x crispa 'Perkeo'

A good subject for the border or a rock garden, this perennial has spikes of deep pink summer flowers rising above the leaves, which emerge with bronze tints in spring. It is ideal for a small garden, and there are more imposing cousins, if space permits.

H: 8 in (20 cm); **S**: 8 in (20 cm)
❄❄❄ ◊ ☀

Astrantia major 'Hadspen Blood'

This reliable perennial has deep blood red flowers in summer that look like pincushions among the elegant green foliage. It spreads rapidly to make excellent ground cover, dying back in winter. Other forms are available with pink or white flowers.

H: 24 in (60 cm); **S**: 18 in (45 cm)
❄❄❄ ◊ ☀

Athyrium niponicum

An elegant fern from Japan, useful for combining with acers and conifers in an Asian scheme with water and rocks. The best forms show silvery markings that make a fine contrast to the purplish stems. It needs neutral to acidic soil to thrive.

H: 8–12 in (20–30 cm); **S**: indefinite
❄❄❄ ◊ ☀ ☀

Aucuba japonica 'Crotonifolia'

It's all too easy to underestimate the sturdy evergreen spotted laurel. The polished leaves retain their golden freckles even in deep shade. The shrub also does well in containers. Red berries sometimes appear on this shrub in the fall.

H: 10 ft (3 m); **S**: 10 ft (3 m)
❄❄❄ ◊ ◊ ☀ ☀

Berberis darwinii

This fine evergreen shrub produces showers of vivid orange flowers in late spring, with blue berries following in fall. Excellent in a large shrub border, it also makes a terrific informal hedge—tight clipping reduces the flowering potential.

H: 10 ft (3 m); **S**: 10 ft (3 m)
❄❄❄ ◊ ☀

Bergenia 'Silberlicht'

Elephant's ears are perennials with tough, shiny leaves. The spring flowers may be white, pink, or red. Those of 'Silberlicht' open white, but age to pale pink. Slow to establish, bergenias eventually reward you with weedproof mats of evergreen foliage.

H: 12–18 in (30–45 cm); **S**: 18–24 in (45–60 cm) ❄❄❄ ◊ ☀

Plant guide (Bo–Ca)

Borago officinalis

Borage is tolerant of dry situations and is one of the few herbs that does well in a shady position. The blue flowers are edible or can be added to drinks. It usually seeds itself freely, often to good effect. *B.* f. *alba* is a desirable form with white flowers.

H: 24 in (60 cm); **S**: 18 in (45 cm)
❋❋❋ ◊ ☼ ☼

Brunnera macrophylla

A good ground-cover perennial for a cool site in shade, hirsute of leaf and with dainty, bright blue forget-me-not-like flowers in spring. Variegated forms are even more valuable. Plants spread rapidly, disappearing underground in winter.

H: 18 in (45 cm); **S**: 24 in (60 cm)
❋❋❋ ◊ ☼ ☼

Buxus sempervirens '*Marginata*'

The classic choice for a low hedge, boxwood is an evergreen shrub of unexpected versatility. Formally clipped specimens can be effective in shade, either in the ground or in containers. Use small plants in window boxes or hanging baskets.

H: up to 15 ft (5 m); **S**: up to 15 ft (5 m)
❋❋❋ ◊ ☼

Camassia leichtlinii

With their tall, elegant spires of mid-spring flowers, these bulbs offer a classy alternative to bluebells in the dappled shade under deciduous trees or among shrubs. For the best effect, plant in bold drifts. Flower colors are shades of smoky blue, or white.

H: 24 in (60 cm); **S**: 4 in (10 cm)
❋❋ ◊ ☼

Camellia '*Cornish Snow*'

One of the first of the camellias to flower, this hybrid shrub has large, single white flowers. It needs acidic soil and shelter from strong winds. Keep plants well watered in fall, when the flower buds are developing. Prune after flowering, if necessary.

H: 10 ft (3 m); **S**: 5 ft (1.5 m)
❋❋❋ ◊ ☼

Camellia japonica '*Tricolor*'

This attractive camellia, an old variety that has stood the test of time, makes a dense, spreading evergreen shrub. The spring flowers are striped in shades of red, pink, or white, no two flowers being exactly the same. Prune after flowering, if necessary.

H: 6 ft (2 m); **S**: 6 ft (2 m) or more
❋❋❋ ◊ ☼

Camellia 'Spring Festival'

Daintier than many other camellias, this cultivar makes a neat pyramid covered in mid- to late spring with small, double, soft pink flowers among the pointed green leaves—a good choice if space is at a premium. A sheltered position is essential.

H: 6–12 ft (2–4 m); **S**: 2–6 ft (0.6–2 m)
❋❋❋ ◊ ☼

Camellia x williamsii 'Donation'

This remains one of the most popular camellias, featuring a profusion of double, soft pink flowers in spring. Later on, the glossy evergreen leaves make a fine backdrop to other plants. To keep it in bounds, give it a light trim after flowering.

H: 15 ft (5 m); **S**: 8 ft (2.5 m)
❋❋❋ ◊ ☼

Campanula glomerata

The clustered bellflower is a useful perennial: coping with most soils and situations and seeding itself freely. The summer flower colors are white and many shades of purplish blue, and cutting plants back after flowering may give a second flush.

H: up to 24 in (60 cm); **S**: indefinite
❋❋❋ ◊ ☼

Campanula poscharskyana

This campanula is commonly seen among rocks or growing out of walls where it has seeded itself, in sun as well as in shade. The clusters of violet-blue flowers are produced over a long period from summer into fall. It appreciates good drainage.

H: 6 in (15 cm); **S**: 24 in (60 cm)
❋❋❋ ◊ ☼

Cardamine pratensis

The cuckoo flower is a perennial with purple, lilac, or white flowers in late spring, offset by glossy decorative foliage. It is a natural woodlander that's equally at home in a cool border, shaded by trees, or a shady rock garden.

H: 12 in (30 cm); **S**: 12 in (30 cm)
❋❋❋ ◊ ☼ ☼

Carex pendula

For an evergreen perennial that provides interest over a long period, the weeping sedge is a good choice, provided the soil is reliably moist. It makes a mound of arching, shiny leaves, with long stems carrying catkinlike flowers from late spring.

H: 4½ ft (1.4 m); **S**: up to 5 ft (1.5 m)
❋❋❋ ◊ ◊ ☼

Plant guide (Ce–Cr)

Ceanothus thyrsiflorus *var.* repens

The California lilac is considered a sun-worshiper, but this evergreen species is a woodlander that tolerates light shade. It may be used as ground cover beneath deciduous trees and will be studded with vivid blue flowers in early summer. It loves dry soil.

H: 3 ft (1 m); **S**: 8 ft (2.5 m)
❀❀❀ ◊ ☀

Clematis alpina

The alpine clematis has dainty blue, bell-like flowers from spring to early summer. Selected forms have flowers in various shades of blue-purple or pink, some being double. Prune after flowering if the plant has accumulated a lot of dead stems.

H: 6–10 ft (2–3 m); **S**: 5 ft (1.5 m)
❀❀❀ ◊ ☀

Clematis 'Fireworks'

This large-flowered clematis is a real dazzler when its luminous violet flowers open in late spring—with a reprise in late summer. Prune lightly in late winter so as not to lose the first flush of flowers. Plants grown into trees are best left unpruned.

H: 6–10 ft (2–3 m); **S**: 3 ft (1 m)
❀❀❀ ◊ ☀

Clematis 'Hagley Hybrid'

Shade suits this large-flowered selection, which tends to bleach with too much sun. There is a touch of blue in the flower, providing a cool contrast to the fresh green leaves in summer. Prune stems to just above the ground in late winter.

H: 6 ft (2 m); **S**: 3 ft (1 m)
❀❀❀ ◊ ☀

Clematis 'Huldine'

This dainty cultivar flowers from mid- to late summer. The white flowers are delicately barred with soft silvery lilac. It is entrancing when allowed to wander through a shrub border. Cut back the stems to 6–12 in (15–30 cm) above ground level in late winter.

H: 10–15 ft (3–5 m); **S**: 6 ft (2 m)
❀❀❀ ◊ ☀

Clematis macropetala

An alternative to *C. alpina*, this species flowers around the same time but with double flowers in white, pink, mauve, or purplish blue. It is excellent on a pillar or grown into a small tree. Prune immediately after flowering, if necessary.

H: 6–10 ft (2–3 m); **S**: 5 ft (1.5 m)
❀❀❀ ◊ ☀

Colchicum speciosum

A sunny spot is often recommended, but this bulb does well in dappled shade provided the leaves receive some direct light between late winter and summer. They die back, allowing the white or pink gobletlike flowers to emerge in naked glory in fall.

H: 7 in (18 cm); **S**: 4 in (10 cm)
❀❀❀ ◊ ☀

Convallaria majalis

The white bell-like flowers of lily-of-the-valley have an unmistakeable scent that hangs on the air in spring. The plant spreads by runners, often invading the cracks in paving. Lovely for picking and worth trying with ferns in a cool rock garden.

H: 9 in (23 cm); **S**: 12 in (30 cm)
❀❀❀ ◊ ☀ ☀

Cornus canadensis

Most of the dogwoods are woody, but this species is a perennial that makes terrific ground cover in shade, ideal if you have a large space to fill. The small white flowers are produced from late spring to early summer, with red berries following in fall.

H: 6 in (15 cm); **S**: indefinite
❀❀❀ ◊ ☀

Corydalis flexuosa

If you want blue in the shade, this is the plant for you. The slender flowers ring out over glassy green foliage from late spring to summer, after which the whole plant disappears underground. It is excellent in a rock garden.

H: 12 in (30 cm); **S**: 8 in (20 cm)
❀❀❀ ◊ ☀

Crocosmia 'Lucifer'

Perhaps the finest of all crocosmias, this robust corm pushes out handsome, pleated leaves in spring. Arching stems carry brilliant red flowers in summer. Lift and separate the corms every two or three years—congested clumps often fail to flower.

H: 3–4 ft (1–1.2 m); **S**: 6 in (15 cm)
❀❀❀ ◊ ☀

Crocus tommasinianus f. albus

Flowering in late winter, plant in quantity to carpet the ground under deciduous trees and shrubs so it completes its growth before these are in full leaf. The species has silvery lilac flowers, but consider more richly colored selections, too.

H: 3–4 in (8–10 cm); **S**: 1 in (2.5 cm)
❀❀❀ ◊ ☀

Plant guide (Cy–Er)

Cyclamen coum
The hardy cyclamen are among the few plants that thrive in the dry shade under trees. This species has heart-shaped leaves, sometimes marked with silver, above which flutter white, pink, or red flowers in winter or early spring. The plant rests over summer.

H: 2–3 in (5–8 cm); **S**: 4 in (10 cm)
❀❀❀ ◊ ☀

Cyclamen hederifolium
This species differs from the preceding one in that the flowers—nearly always pink—appear in fall before the leaves emerge. The foliage, often exquisitely patterned, is a feature throughout the winter. The plant self-seeds freely.

H: 4–5 in (10–13 cm); **S**: 6 in (15 cm)
❀❀❀ ◊ ☀

Daphne laureola
Lacking the knockout scent of some of its cousins, this daphne is valued nevertheless for its tolerance of deep shade. The yellowish green flowers are produced from late winter to early spring among the evergreen leaves on a neat-growing shrub.

H: 3 ft (1 m); **S**: 5 ft (1.5 m)
❀❀❀ ◊ ☀ ☀

Darmera peltata
A fine thing to edge a stream or large pond, this robust plant pushes out sturdy stems topped with bright pink or white flowers in spring. The umbrella-like leaves then expand, supplying a strong architectural presence throughout the summer.

H: 6 ft (2 m); **S**: 3 ft (1 m)
❀❀❀ ◊ ◖ ☀

Dicentra spectabilis
Bleeding heart has charming, locket-like pink flowers that dangle in a row from colorful stems in mid- to late spring. The white form, *D. f. alba*, is slightly sturdier. Both are excellent in light woodland or among large rocks. Plants are dormant in winter.

H: 4 ft (1.2 m); **S**: 18 in (45 cm)
❀❀❀ ◊ ◖ ☀

Dicksonia antarctica
The tree fern is much used by designers to introduce a tropical touch. It's very slow-growing, so for immediate impact, look for larger specimens with well-developed trunks. Water copiously in summer if the soil looks like it is drying out.

H: 6 ft (2 m) or more; **S**: 6 ft (2 m)
❀❀ ◊ ◖ ☀ ☀

Digitalis purpurea
Foxgloves are excellent in woodland, where their spires of thimblelike flowers emerge from the shadows, or in borders. They come in a wide color range, including a delicious soft apricot. Foxgloves are biennial, flowering in their second year.

H: 3–4 ft (1–1.2 m); **S**: 12 in (30 cm)
❄❄❄ ◊ ◖ ☼

Dodecatheon pulchellum
Shooting stars are herbaceous perennials with rosettes of oval leaves and from mid- to late spring produce cyclamen-like deep pink flowers with swept-back petals. A great choice for a shady rock garden, but remember that plants die down after flowering.

H: 14 in (35 cm); **S**: 6 in (15 cm)
❄❄❄ ◊ ◖ ☀

Dryopteris filix-mas
The male fern is good choice for a woodland garden, with tall, upright, feathery, light green fronds. Though technically deciduous, plants do not die back completely in fall. Selected forms have crisped or crested fronds.

H: 3 ft (1 m); **S**: 3 ft (1 m)
❄❄❄ ◖ ◖ ☀

Elaeagnus x ebbingei 'Limelight'
A good plant for a coastal garden, and excellent for hedging, this shrub has evergreen leaves, speckled with pewter gray, that develop yellow and pale green central splashes. The creamy white fall flowers are inconspicuous but sweetly scented.

H: 10 ft (3 m); **S**: 10 ft (3 m)
❄❄❄ ◊ ◖

Epimedium grandiflorum
This perennial spreads to form mats of heart-shaped green leaves. Dainty white, yellow, pink, or purple flowers are held on wiry stems from mid- to late spring. To show them off to full advantage, shear back the old leaves in late winter.

H: 8–12 in (20–30 cm); **S**: 12 in (30 cm)
❄❄❄ ◊ ◖

Eranthis hyemalis
The winter aconite is usually the first of the bulbs to appear at the turn of the year, opening its golden buttercup-like flowers as the sun filters through the bare branches of deciduous trees and shrubs. It colonizes, but takes its time.

H: 2–3 in (5–8 cm); **S**: 2 in (5 cm)
❄❄❄ ◊ ◖

Plant guide (Er–Ge)

Erythronium dens-canis

The dog's-tooth violet is one of the delights of the spring woodland garden, though its presence above ground is fleeting. White, pink, or purple flowers with swept-back petals are produced singly on wiry stems above beautifully marbled leaves.

H: 4–6 in (10–15 cm); **S**: 4 in (10 cm)
❄❄❄ ◊ ☼

Erythronium 'Pagoda'

This hybrid is bigger in all its parts than the preceding species, with nodding yellow flowers in late spring and broad, mottled, glossy green leaves. Grow it in clumps around deciduous trees and shrubs or in a rock garden.

H: 6–14 in (15–35 cm); **S**: 6 in (15 cm)
❄❄❄ ◊ ☼

Euonymus fortunei cultivars

These evergreen shrubs are grown for their variegated leaves and provide useful fillers in borders. They make reasonably compact mounds that are tolerant of clipping, or plants can be persuaded to climb a wall. Prune out plain green shoots as they are seen.

H: 3 ft (1 m); **S**: 6 ft (2 m)
❄❄❄ ◊ ☼

Euphorbia amygdaloides

The wood spurge is a perennial that spreads rapidly to colonize shady areas. Above rosettes of dark green leaves, heads of lime green flowers stand on short stems in spring. This plant can be invasive, but is excellent ground cover in problem areas.

H: 30 in (75 cm); **S**: 12 in (30 cm)
❄❄❄ ◗ ☼

x Fatshedera lizei

A hybrid of ivy and *Fatsia*, commonly grown as a houseplant, this shrub can be used to bring a touch of drama to a shady site with its shiny, evergreen leaves. Or you can train it up a wall, pillar, or even a tree. Some forms have variegated foliage.

H: 6 ft (2 m) or more; **S**: to 10 ft (3 m)
❄❄❄ ◊ ☼

Fritillaria meleagris

The snake's-head fritillary is a quiet plant with checkered, dull purple lampshadelike flowers in mid-spring. It appreciates soil that does not dry out in summer and is excellent for naturalizing in damp grass. There is also an appealing white form.

H: 10 in (25 cm); **S**: 2–3 in (5–8 cm)
❄❄❄ ◗ ◗ ☼

Fuchsia 'Lady Thumb'

There are many hardy fuchsias, nearly all of which are suitable for growing in light shade. This is a tried-and-tested variety with red and white flowers over a long period. Larger hybrids can be trained against walls or as standards.

H: up to 12 in (30 cm); **S**: up to 18 in (45 cm) ❄❄ ◊ ☀

Fuchsia magellanica *var.* molinae

This pale pink fuchsia, known as lady's eardrops, can be grown as a freestanding shrub but is easily trained against a shady wall or on a pillar. The flowers, dainty as fairy lights, appear over a long period from midsummer until the frosts.

H: 6 ft (2 m); **S**: 6 ft (2 m) ❄❄ ◊ ☀

Galanthus nivalis

Harbingers of spring, snowdrops are essential for the winter garden. Best grown beneath deciduous trees, on banks or among shrubs, the common snowdrop, with its bell-like white flowers, does well in heavy soil. Lift and divide every year after flowering.

H: 4 in (10 cm); **S**: 2 in (5 cm) ❄❄❄ ◊ ☀

Garrya elliptica

This evergreen shrub is valued for its long, pinkish silver, tassel-like catkins that dangle from the stems in late winter, persisting well into spring. It is perfect as an informal wall shrub. Indeed, shelter of this kind is essential in cold regions to protect it from frost.

H: 12 ft (4 m); **S**: 12 ft (4 m) ❄❄❄ ◊ ☀

Geranium macrorrhizum

This geranium has the advantage of scented leaves, and liverish-purple flowers that open in mid-spring. There are also a number of selected forms with paler flowers. Like most of the hardy geraniums, it makes splendid ground cover.

H: 20 in (50 cm); **S**: 24 in (60 cm) ❄❄❄ ◊ ◊ ☀

Geranium phaeum 'Album'

The mourning widow is a real woodland plant. The species has dark purple mid-spring flowers that hang from stems over chocolate-purple leaves. It hybridizes freely with the white 'Album' (*above*) to produce plants with soft mauve flowers.

H: 32 in (80 cm); **S**: 18 in (45 cm) ❄❄❄ ◊ ◊ ☀ ☀

Plant guide (Hedera)

Hedera colchica '*Sulphur Heart*'
If you are looking for an evergreen climber to provide year-round interest, this form of the Persian ivy should come high on the list. Its large leaves are generously splashed with warm creamy yellow. Quick-growing, it may also be used as ground cover.

H: 15 ft (5 m); **S**: 15 ft (5 m)
❄❄❄ ◊ ◗ ☼

Hedera helix '*Adam*'
This form of common ivy has glacial-looking mint green leaves that are delicately margined with white. Not overly vigorous, this ivy therefore makes a good choice for a container if trimmed to keep it neat.

H: up to 15 ft (5 m); **S**: up to 10 ft (3 m)
❄❄❄ ◊ ◗ ☼

Hedera helix '*Erecta*'
Something of a curiosity among the ivies, this is a shrubby plant rather than a climber, producing upright spikes of rounded, mid-green leaves in tiers. It is a fine addition to any shade planting, especially where space is limited, or to a rock garden.

H: 3 ft (1 m); **S**: 18 in (30 cm)
❄❄❄ ◊ ◗ ☼ ☀

Hedera helix '*Glacier*'
This ivy looks as cool as its name suggests, with small gray-green leaves variegated with silver and cream. It's a versatile plant that may be used on a shady wall, as ground cover beneath trees, or in containers and hanging baskets.

H: 6 ft (2 m); **S**: 3 ft (1 m)
❄❄❄ ◊ ◗ ☼

Hedera helix '*Goldheart*'
This ivy has shiny green leaves that are generously splashed with rich golden yellow. Without sufficient light, it tends to lose its variegation, so cut out any plain green growth. It sometimes masquerades under the name 'Oro di Bogliasco'.

H: 25 ft (8 m); **S**: 12 ft (4 m)
❄❄❄ ◊ ◗ ☼

Hedera helix '*Green Ripple*'
The leaves on this selection are larger than those of some of the other common ivies and have jagged, pointed edges. This effect is best observed where the ivy is grown against a wall, adding texture to the flat surface.

H: 6 ft (2 m); **S**: 3 ft (1 m)
❄❄❄ ◊ ◗ ☼ ☀

Hedera helix '*Ivalace*'

The glossy green leaves of this ivy are wavy or crimped at the edges and marked with light green veins. Plant it against a low wall or as ground cover, or use it as a trailer in hanging baskets and containers as a foil to more flamboyantly colored plants.

H: 3 ft (1 m); **S**: 3 ft (1 m)
❄❄❄ ◊ ◊ ☼ ☀

Hedera helix '*Little Diamond*'

One of the prettiest of the ivies, compact and with diamond-shaped leaves, as its name suggests. The basic leaf color is a patchy gray-green, with broad cream variegation at the edges. A good plant for a rock garden, container, or basket.

H: 12 in (30 cm); **S**: 12 in (30 cm)
❄❄❄ ◊ ◊ ☼

Hedera helix '*Parsley Crested*'

The appeal of this ivy is in the rounded, wavy-edged foliage. It makes an excellent choice, adding color and texture to a wall or fence in deep shade. The plant is sometimes sold under the alternative name 'Cristata'.

H: 6 ft (2 m); **S**: 3 ft (1 m)
❄❄ ◊ ◊ ☼ ☀

Hedera helix '*Pedata*'

The elongated lobes of each leaf on 'Pedata' have given rise to its common name—bird's-foot ivy. A vigorous plant, it will create a beautiful dark green screen when grown on a wall or fence behind a shady border. It is sometimes listed as 'Caenwoodiana'.

H: 12 ft (4 m); **S**: 6 ft (2 m)
❄❄❄ ◊ ◊ ☼ ☀

Hedera helix '*Pittsburgh*'

This compact ivy has relatively large lobed leaves in relation to the size of the plant. It grows to form a thick mat of foliage, and is a good choice as a filler in a container, hanging basket, or window box. Planted *en masse*, it makes good ground cover.

H: 3 ft (1 m); **S**: 3 ft (1 m)
❄❄ ◊ ◊ ☼ ☀

Hedera hibernica '*Sulphurea*'

Irish ivy is a vigorous plant with large leaves, perfect if you have plenty of space to fill. This selection is less invasive, with grayish-green leaves that are marked with pale sulfur yellow, making a good foil for smaller-leaved ivies.

H: 10 ft (3 m); **S**: 5 ft (1.5 m)
❄❄❄ ◊ ◊ ☼ ☀

Plant guide (He–Ho)

Helleborus orientalis
Lenten hellebores are fine evergreen perennials for late winter to early spring interest, with cup-shaped flowers in a range of colors—white, cream, pinkish red, and a dramatic purple. Double forms are equally desirable. They do well in heavy soil.

H: 18 in (45 cm); **S**: 18 in (45 cm)
❀❀❀ ◊ ◐ ☀

Hemerocallis 'Corky'
Most daylilies are sun-lovers, but this variety tolerates some shade. It's an evergreen perennial with strappy, grasslike leaves and clear yellow trumpetlike flowers in midsummer. The flowers last only a day but are produced in succession.

H: 28 in (70 cm); **S**: 16 in (40 cm)
❀❀❀ ◊ ◐ ☀

Hemerocallis 'Golden Chimes'
The flowers of this daylily are broad and deep yellow, with petals that curve gently backward, opening from reddish brown buds in early summer. The narrow, grassy leaves are a feature throughout the year, and it is an excellent border perennial.

H: 36 in (90 cm); **S**: 18 in (45 cm)
❀❀❀ ◊ ◐ ☀

Hepatica acutiloba
The hepaticas are related to the anemones and enjoy similar conditions. This species is a modest plant for woodland or a rock garden, with five-petaled blue, pink, or white flowers in early spring. It thrives in heavy, preferably alkaline, soil.

H: 3 in (8 cm); **S**: 6 in (15 cm)
❀❀❀ ◊ ◐ ☀

Heuchera micrantha var. diversifolia 'Palace Purple'
This plant's best feature is its metallic bronze-red leaves. In early summer, salmon pink flowers rise above them on wiry stems. The plant spreads to form good ground cover. If grown in deep shade, it needs moist soil.

H: 18–24 in (45–60 cm); **S**: 18–24 in (45–60 cm) ❀❀❀ ◊ ◐ ☀ ☀

x Heucherella tiarelloides
Hybridizing *Heuchera* and *Tiarella* results in robust shade-lovers that are very good as ground cover or border plants. The leaves can show brown markings as they emerge. Plumes of tiny pink flowers wave above them from mid-spring to early summer.

H: 18 in (45 cm); **S**: 18 in (45 cm)
❀❀❀ ◊ ◐ ☀ ☀

Hosta 'Green Fountain'

This distinctive and elegant hosta has thin-textured leaves of a clear, shining green that would easily scorch in sun. They are held upright but cascade downward at the tips. Pale mauve flowers are produced in summer. Effective slug control is essential.

H: 18 in (45 cm); **S**: 3 ft (1 m)
❄❄❄ ◊ ◖ ☼ ☀

Hosta 'Halcyon'

The leaves of 'Halcyon' are thick and heart-shaped when mature, and covered in a wax that makes them appear gray-blue. Lavender-gray flowers appear in summer. Shade enhances the blue in the leaf of this hosta, one of the best of its kind.

H: 16 in (40 cm); **S**: 28 in (70 cm)
❄❄❄ ◊ ◖ ☼ ☀

Hosta 'Krossa Regal'

Its vase-shaped habit makes this an unmistakable plant among the gray-leaved hostas. The summer flowers are pale lilac. Like all the hostas, it makes terrific ground cover, but to appreciate its distinctive form to the fullest, grow it in a large container.

H: 28 in (70 cm); **S**: 30 in (75 cm)
❄❄❄ ◊ ◖ ☼ ☀

Hosta 'Love Pat'

This hosta has thick and rounded, heart-shaped, puckered leaves that curve almost into a cup shape. Off-white bell-shaped flowers appear in summer. More slug-resistant than many hostas, it is an excellent border plant, if rather slow to establish.

H: 18 in (45 cm); **S**: 3 ft (1 m)
❄❄❄ ◊ ◖ ☼ ☀

Hosta 'Sagae'

One of the most dramatic of all the hostas, this selection makes a clump of thick-textured, almost blackish-green leaves thinly margined with creamy yellow. In summer, tall stems carry small, funnel-shaped lavender-white flowers. Slow to establish.

H: 3 ft (1 m); **S**: 3 ft (1 m)
❄❄❄ ◊ ◖ ☼ ☀

Hosta 'Sum and Substance'

This hosta has leaves like chamois leather, thick-textured with an almost felty appearance. Unusually for this shade-loving genus, it tolerates sun—indeed, some sun is needed to bring out the warm yellow-green coloring. Summer flowers are almost white.

H: 30 in (75 cm); **S**: 4 ft (1.2 m)
❄❄❄ ◊ ◖ ☼

Plant guide (Hy–Li)

Hyacinthoides non-scripta
Bluebells are natural woodlanders, carpeting the ground with blue in mid-spring just after the daffodils have finished. Individually, they are rather spindly plants and are best seen *en masse*. Cut back the flowers as they fade to prevent self-seeding.

H: 8–16 in (20–40 cm); **S**: 3 in (8 cm)
❋ ❋ ❋ ◊ ☀

Hydrangea anomala *subsp.* petiolaris
This self-clinging climber grows in quite deep shade, producing large heads of creamy white flowers in early summer. It is slow to get going, and large specimens are of great age. Pruning is best kept to a minimum.

H: up to 50 ft (15 m); **S**: up to 20 ft (6 m)
❋ ❋ ❋ ◊ ☀ ☀

Hydrangea macrophylla
Hydrangeas are essential shrubs for shade. Flower colors include white, pink (in alkaline soil), and blue (in acidic). The flowers are "mophead" (clusters of flowers) or "lacecap" (large flowers around a cluster of smaller ones). Prune in spring.

H: 5 ft (1.5 m); **S**: 4 ft (1.2 m)
❋ ❋ ❋ ◊ ☀

Hydrangea villosa
This rather gaunt shrub is grown mainly for its velvety green leaves and peeling bark. The lacecap bluish purple flowers, which open in late summer, are a bonus. It appreciates some shelter. Plants may become treelike with age.

H: up to 12 ft (4 m); **S**: up to 12 ft (4 m) ❋ ❋ ❋ ◊ ☀

Hypericum 'Hidcote'
This evergreen shrub earns its place in gardens by virtue of its toughness and reliability. Gleaming yellow, cup-shaped flowers open from midsummer to early fall, and the leaves are pleasantly aromatic. It's good in a shrub or mixed border.

H: 4 ft (1.2 m); **S**: 5 ft (1.5 m)
❋ ❋ ❋ ◊ ☀

Impatiens schlechteri
Of the annuals that grow well in shade, busy Lizzies are among the most valuable. The white, pink, orange, or red flowers are produced over a long season from summer to fall. They are essential for containers and hanging baskets.

H: 14 in (35 cm); **S**: 12 in (30 cm)
❀ ◊ ☀

Iris pseudacorus

Yellow flag iris is a water plant for the margins of a pond or stream. The swordlike, bright green leaves have a strong architectural quality, and are enlivened by yellow flowers from late spring to early summer. Restrain this spreading iris in an aquatic basket.

H: 1–3 ft (0.9–1.5 m); **S**: 24 in (60 cm)
❄❄❄ ◐ ● ☀

Kirengeshoma palmata

This clump-forming perennial would probably be better known were it not for its insistence on nonalkaline soil. Wiry stalks carry elegant, lanternlike pale yellow flowers from late summer to fall above large palm-shaped pale green leaves.

H: 2–4 ft (0.6–1.2 m); **S**: 30 in (75 cm)
❄❄❄ ◐ ☀

Lamium maculatum '*Beacon Silver*'

Deadnettle is one of the few perennials that thrives in the dry shade beneath trees. 'Beacon Silver' may be relied on to form mats of shining pewter leaves in areas where few other plants grow.

H: 8 in (20 cm); **S**: 3 ft (1 m)
❄❄❄ ○ ☀ ☀

Lathyrus latifolius

The perennial pea looks much like the annual sweet pea, but minus the scent. It emerges every spring, and produces magenta flowers all summer. Allow it to ramble through spring-flowering shrubs. 'White Pearl' is a desirable white-flowered form.

H: 6 ft (2 m); **S**: 3 ft (1 m) or more
❄❄❄ ○ ☀

Leucojum aestivum

Snowflakes, flowering at the same time as daffodils, are rather less commonly grown bulbs, but make an elegant addition to plantings, with their graceful stems and bell-like white flowers. They thrive in heavy soil that stays moist.

H: 18–24 in (45–60 cm); **S**: 3 in (8 cm)
❄❄❄ ◐ ☀

Ligularia '*The Rocket*'

A robust plant with a wonderful sculptural quality, ideal for reliably moist soil. Tall blackish stems set with bright yellow flowers shoot skyward in summer above jagged-edged leaves. It looks good by water or toward the back of a border.

H: 6 ft (1.8 m); **S**: 3 ft (1 m)
❄❄❄ ◐ ☀

Plant guide (Lilium)

Lilium *Bellingham Group*

These old hybrids provide points of color in light woodland from early to midsummer. The turkscap flowers vary in color—yellow, orange, and red—but all are attractively spotted with brown. For the best effect, plant in groups. They need acidic soil.

H: 6 ft (1.8 m); **S**: 10 in (25 cm)
❄❄❄ ◊ ☼

Lilium henryi

Vigorous and easy to grow, this lily has warm apricot yellow turkscap flowers that are spotted with black. The tall stems benefit from staking unless the bulbs are planted among lower-growing shrubs for support. It needs neutral to alkaline soil.

H: to 6 ft (2 m); **S**: 10 in (25 cm)
❄❄❄ ◊ ☼

Lilium lancifolium

The tiger lily needs no introduction, with its turkscap, bright orange late summer flowers dramatically spotted with black. To increase stocks, snap off the bulbils that are scattered up the stems. It prefers, though does not insist on, nonalkaline soil.

H: 5 ft (1.5 m); **S**: 10 in (25 cm)
❄❄❄ ◐ ☼

Lilium longiflorum

The Easter or Bermuda lily is one of the easiest to grow, but needs protection from frost. In cold areas, grow it in containers. The trumpet-like, scented white flowers, often grown for cutting, open around midsummer. It tolerates alkaline soil.

H: 3 ft (1 m); **S**: 10 in (25 cm)
❄ ◊ ☼

Lilium martagon

The martagon lily, a favorite cottage garden plant, is one of the oldest in cultivation. From early to midsummer, each stem can hold up to 50 small, pinkish purple turkscap flowers. It does well in both acidic and alkaline soils, provided they are well drained.

H: 3–6 ft (0.9–2 m); **S**: 8 in (20 cm)
❄❄❄ ◊ ☼

Lilium martagon *var.* album

This form of the preceding plant has glassy green stems and pure white flowers that hang from them in summer. It is good for lightening a shady spot beneath deciduous trees. Another variant is *Lilium m.* var. *cattaniae*, with maroon flowers.

H: 3–6 ft (0.9–2 m); **S**: 8 in (20 cm)
❄❄❄ ◊ ☼

Lilium medeoloides

This is a good lily for a small garden or container. The turkscap, orange-red to apricot flowers, spotted darker, are produced in midsummer, while the leaves are set around the stems like spokes, giving rise to its common name, wheel lily. It needs acidic soil.

H: 16–30 in (40–75 cm); **S**: 8 in (20 cm)
❋❋❋ ◊ ☀

Lilium nepalense

A beautiful lily, unfortunately not hardy, that throws up erect or arching stems with greenish yellow flowers stained with purple inside. In cool areas, grow in large containers as the underground stems tend to grow horizontally. It needs acidic soil.

H: 4 ft (1.2 m); **S**: 10 in (25 cm)
❋ ◊ ☀

Lilium pardalinum

The leopard or panther lily produces unscented turkscap flowers. Bright orange-red with dark brown spots—some of the spots haloed in yellow—they hang from the stems in summer. Ideal for the back of a border, it tolerates alkalinity, but not dry soil.

H: 5–8 ft (1.5–2.5 m); **S**: 12 in (30 cm)
❋❋❋ ◊ ☀

Lilium pyrenaicum

Virtually indestructible, this easy lily quickly produces offsets underground that create clumps. The curious scent of the lemon yellow turkscap flowers is a bit offputting, so plant toward the back of a border or under deciduous trees. It needs neutral to alkaline soil.

H: 2–4 ft (0.6–1.2 m); **S**: 10 in (25 cm)
❋❋❋ ◊ ☀

Lilium speciosum

This Japanese lily is one of the last to flower—at the tail end of summer—releasing a heavy scent that hangs on the air. The large turkscap flowers are spotted with deeper pink or crimson. *L. speciosum* var. *album* has pure white flowers. Both need acidic soil.

H: 3–6 ft (1–1.8 m); **S**: 10 in (25 cm)
❋❋❋ ◊ ☀

Lilium superbum

The American turkscap lily is valued for its late season, flowering in late summer and early fall. Tall stems carry unscented, bright orange flowers that are flushed with red, and spotted with maroon and green toward the bases. It needs acidic soil.

H: 5–10 ft (1.5–3 m); **S**: 12 in (30 cm)
❋❋❋ ◊ ☀

Plant guide (Lo–Os)

Lobelia erinus

This is one of few annuals that do well in shade. Compact forms make good bedding and trailers are virtually indispensable in summer baskets. Snip off faded blooms and the plants flower into fall. Red, pink, and white forms are also available.

H: 6 in (15 cm); **S**: 6 in (15 cm)
❄ ◊ ◌ ☀

Lonicera x tellmanniana

All the climbing honeysuckles are natural woodlanders, and this hybrid can be relied on to light up a shady corner when its clusters of rich orange trumpetlike flowers open in early summer. Prune out congested stems in late winter as necessary.

H: 15 ft (5 m); **S**: 10 ft (3 m)
❄❄❄ ◊ ☀

Lunaria annua

Honesty is a charming cottage garden biennial, grown as much for its silvery fall seedheads as its white or purple spring flowers. New plants are easily raised from seed sown in spring or fall, but you may also find self-sown seedlings in the garden.

H: 36 in (90 cm); **S**: 12 in (30 cm)
❄❄❄ ◊ ☀

Lysichiton americanus

The skunk cabbage is a grand perennial that needs space, ideally in damp ground alongside a stream. After the brilliant yellow spathes have died back in late spring, the glossy leaves continue to expand to make an imposing statement.

H: 3 ft (1 m); **S**: 4 ft (1.2 m)
❄❄❄ ◊ ◌ ☀

Lysimachia nummularia 'Aurea'

Creeping Jenny, of which this is a yellow-leaved form, makes terrific ground cover. It may also be used to trail in hanging baskets or around the edges of large containers. The cup shaped summer flowers are bright golden yellow.

H: 2 in (5 cm); **S**: indefinite
❄❄❄ ◊ ◌ ☀

Matteuccia struthiopteris

The ostrich or shuttlecock fern is a deciduous species with long, tapering fronds that create an elegant, vaselike structure. The rootstock spreads rapidly underground to create colonies of new plants. It needs neutral to acidic soil.

H: 5½ ft (1.7 m); **S**: 3 ft (1 m)
❄❄❄ ◊ ☀

Milium effusum 'Aureum'

Bowles' golden grass is an essential perennial that holds its yellow color all through the summer. It runs happily around early flowering plants, such as primulas and dwarf bulbs, without ever swamping them, always creating pleasing pictures.

H: 18 in (45 cm); **S**: 12 in (30 cm)
❅❅❅ ◊ ☀

Narcissus 'Acatea'

If you cannot grow—or do not like—tulips, substitute this late daffodil, whose sparkling white flowers light up the shade—with the added bonus of a delicious scent. Cut off the flowers as they fade to help build up the bulb for flowering the next year.

H: 18 in (45 cm); **S**: 4 in (10 cm)
❅❅❅ ◊ ◑ ☀

Narcissus 'Jumblie'

Excellent in borders, containers, and window boxes, dwarf daffodils are much sturdier than their diminutive stature suggests. 'Jumblie' produces quantities of bright golden yellow flowers with petals that sweep back from the trumpets.

H: 7 in (17 cm); **S**: 2 in (5 cm)
❅❅❅ ◊ ☀

Narcissus 'Tête-à-tête'

One of the most popular of the early-flowering daffodils, with dainty, clear yellow flowers. Plant in clumps among shrubs or in the lawn, or mix with small evergreen shrubs in winter containers or window boxes. The flowers are good for picking.

H: 6 in (15 cm); **S**: 2 in (5 cm)
❅❅❅ ◊ ☀

Ophiopogon planiscapus 'Nigrescens'

An evergreen perennial grasslike plant that appeals to designers, as its leaves are virtually black. It makes a splendid foil to a huge range of flowering plants, but it prefers acidic soil. It does well in a container.

H: 8 in (20 cm); **S**: 12 in (30 cm)
❅❅❅ ◊ ☀

Osmunda regalis

Handsome in a large container—provided it's well watered—the royal fern is also a fine specimen for water-side planting. The deep green fronds have a tough, leathery texture and, in summer, change into long, narrow masses of brownish spore capsules.

H: 6 ft (2 m); **S**: 12 ft (4 m)
❅❅❅ ◖ ☀

Plant guide (Pa–Po)

Pachyphragma macrophyllum
In spring, this semievergreen perennial has clusters of white flowers above the glossy, rounded leaves, followed by heart-shaped fruits. Good for ground cover under deciduous trees or among shrubs, but slow growing.

H: up to 16 in (40 cm); **S**: up to 36 in (90 cm) ❄❄❄ ◊ ☀

Pachysandra terminalis
This evergreen perennial is essentially a foliage plant, grown for its glossy green leaves that provide good cover under trees or among shrubs. The clusters of white flowers in spring are small in relation to the plant. 'Variegata' has white-edged leaves.

H: 8 in (20 cm); **S**: indefinite ❄❄❄ ◊ ◊ ◑ ☀

Paeonia lactiflora 'Duchesse de Nemours'
The herbaceous peonies are excellent perennials for light shade. This hybrid has large, double, whipped cream flowers with a rich, spicy fragrance. Peonies resent disturbance but are usually long-lived.

H: 32 in (80 cm); **S**: 32 in (80 cm) ❄❄❄ ◊ ◑

Paeonia lutea
This tree peony is grown as much for its handsome jade green leaves as for its cup-shaped, gleaming buttercup-yellow flowers that fleetingly appear among them in late spring. Keep pruning to a minimum. Shelter from strong winds is essential.

H: 5 ft (1.5 m); **S**: 5 ft (1.5 m) ❄❄❄ ◊ ☀

Paeonia suffruticosa 'Nigata Akashigata'
Tree peonies offer a fleeting week of pleasure in late spring when the swollen buds open into sumptuous flowers. In this hybrid, they are pale pink, with a deep magenta stripe. Plants benefit from regular fertilizing.

H: 6 ft (2 m); **S**: 6 ft (2 m) ❄❄❄ ◊ ☀

Philadelphus coronarius 'Aureus'
Some sunlight is needed to bring out the color of this mock orange's brilliant yellow leaves, but too much results in scorch. Plant where the shrub will be shaded between midday and late afternoon. Cloyingly scented cream flowers appear in early summer.

H: 8 ft (2.5 m); **S**: 5 ft (1.5 m) ❄❄❄ ◊ ◑

Phlox stolonifera
Creeping phlox is a natural woodlander, with trailing stems that carry starlike pale to deep purple flowers in early summer. It looks good at the edge of a shady border or raised bed. 'Ariane' *(below)* is a white-flowered selection.

H: 4–6 in (10–15 cm); **S**: 12 in (30 cm)
❀❀❀ ◊ ☼

Pieris '*Forest Flame*'
This evergreen shrub truly deserves its name, producing brilliant coral red leaves in late winter to early spring. Floppy plumes of lily-of-the-valley-like flowers appear in mid-spring. It must have acidic soil. If yours is alkaline, grow it in a container.

H: 12 ft (4 m); **S**: 6 ft (2 m)
❀❀ ◊ ☼

Polemonium caeruleum
Jacob's ladder is an excellent border perennial with arching leaves and sky blue (or, rarely, white), funnel-shaped flowers in early summer. It is also effective in a wildflower meadow. The topgrowth dies back completely in winter.

H: up to 36 in (90 cm); **S**: 12 in (30 cm) ❀❀❀ ◊ ☼

Polygonatum x hybridum
Solomon's seal enlivens dank, shady corners in mid-spring with arching stems hung with lightly scented white bells. After flowering, the perennial is often skeletonized by Solomon's seal sawfly larvae, but the pest seldom causes outright death.

H: 5 ft (1.5 m); **S**: 12 in (30 cm)
❀❀❀ ◊ ☼ ☀

Polypodium vulgare
The evergreen common polypody is a useful plant, adapting to a range of conditions but preferring stony soil. It has smooth, leathery, deeply cut, lance-shaped green fronds set on either side of a central stem. Selected forms have variously cut fronds.

H: 12 in (30 cm); **S**: indefinite
❀❀❀ ◊ ☼

Polystichum setiferum
The evergreen soft shield fern is an elegant plant with gracefully arching, lance-shaped dark green fronds. With adequate shade—it will even grow happily in deep shade—and moisture, it may produce large clumps. Selected forms have more finely cut fronds.

H: 4 ft (1.2 m); **S**: 36 in (90 cm)
❀❀❀ ◊ ☼ ☀

Plant guide (Pr–Ro)

Primula bulleyana

This primula is one of a number of species referred to as candelabra, because of the tiered arrangement of the orange flowers up the stems. The spring blooms appear above clumps of soft green leaves. It needs neutral to acidic soil that does not dry out.

H: 24 in (60 cm); **S**: 24 in (60 cm)
❄❄❄ ◐ ♦ ☀

Primula denticulata

Blooming from mid-spring to summer, drumstick primulas are like mini alliums, with balls of purple or white flowers on top of stout stems, which shoot up from a rosette of spoon-shaped leaves. Excellent by a stream or at the edge of a border.

H: 18 in (45 cm); **S**: 18 in (45 cm)
❄❄❄ ◐ ☀

Primula polyanthus

Polyanthus bring a flash of jewel-like color to late winter and spring gardens. They are perennial, but are usually treated as annuals, since flowers on old plants tend to be smaller and paler. Use in borders or baskets, and discard after flowering.

H: 6 in (15 cm); **S**: 8 in (20 cm)
❄❄❄ ○ ◐ ☀

Primula veris

Cowslips are pretty little meadow plants with bright yellow spring flowers. Attractive studding a lawn or, even better, a bank, and appreciating heavy, moisture-retentive soil, they can also be used in a border or window box.

H: 10 in (25 cm); **S**: 10 in (25 cm)
❄❄❄ ◐ ☀

Pulmonaria 'Sissinghurst White'

Despite their coarse appearance, lungwort leaves are sensitive to too much sunlight. After the flowers have finished—from late spring—the leaves continue to expand, luxuriating in cool shade. Other varieties have pink, red, or blue flowers.

H: 12 in (30 cm); **S**: 18 in (45 cm)
❄❄❄ ○ ◐ ☀

Rheum palmatum 'Atrosanguineum'

Chinese rhubarb is a grand foliage plant for damp soil, with its imposing leaves that emerge crimson purple, gradually becoming more green. In summer, it has numerous tiny, rich cerise-pink flowers.

H: 8 ft (2.5 m); **S**: 6 ft (1.8 m)
❄❄❄ ◐ ☀

Rhododendron luteum

This vigorous, deciduous species is the parent of many hybrids, some of which have inherited the fragrance of its bright yellow flowers, produced from late spring to early summer. The leaves turn scarlet before dropping in fall. Grow in acidic soil.

H: 12 ft (4 m); **S**: 12 ft (4 m)
❄❄❄ ◊ ☀

Rhododendron 'Palestrina'

Among the evergreen azaleas, this hybrid stands out for its compact habit and free-flowering nature. The trusses of pure white flowers, produced in late spring, contrast vividly with the rich green leaves. Acidic soil is required.

H: 4 ft (1.2 m); **S**: 4 ft (1.2 m)
❄❄❄ ◊ ☀

Rhododendron 'Persil'

This deciduous azalea makes a bushy shrub suitable for light woodland, toward the back of a border, or for a large container. The clusters of mid-spring flowers are pure white, with a pronounced yellow-orange flare inside. It must have acidic soil.

H: 6 ft (2 m); **S**: 6 ft (2 m)
❄❄❄ ◊ ☀

Rodgersia sambucifolia

This stately perennial is ideal for a bog garden or streamside, but will also do well in shady borders, where its chestnutlike leaves make a dramatic foil to other plants. Frothy panicles of white or pink flowers are carried on tall stems in midsummer.

H: 6 ft (2 m); **S**: 3 ft (1 m)
❄❄❄ ◐ ☀

Rosa 'Albéric Barbier'

This old rambling rose is a good choice for a shady wall. In early summer it is covered with endearingly scruffy, whipped cream flowers that have a light scent. In a mild winter, it will also hang on to its leaves. Prune after flowering, if necessary.

H: 15 ft (5 m); **S**: 10 ft (3 m)
❄❄❄ ◊ ☀

Rosa 'Mermaid'

A climbing rose unlike any other. The large, single, creamy yellow flowers seldom cover the plant, but open over a long period from early summer to late fall. In a mild winter, the plant may retain its leaves. Slow to establish but worth the wait.

H: 20 ft (6 m); **S**: 20 ft (6 m)
❄❄❄ ◊ ☀

Plant guide (Ro–Ti)

Rosa 'New Dawn'
This popular climber's flowers emerge a little later than many others, but then continue well into fall. Silvery pink, they have a light, spicy fragrance. The stems are stiff and thorny, so should be tied in to their support while still young and flexible.

H: 10 ft (3 m); **S**: 8 ft (2.5 m)
❀❀❀ ◊ ☀

Rosa rugosa
A tough, tolerant shrub rose that does well in a number of situations, including dry soil. The large, single, pink or white summer flowers that appear among the crinkly leaves are sweetly scented. They are followed by tomato-like, vivid orange-red fruits.

H: 3–8 ft (1–2.5 m); **S**: 3–8 ft (1–2.5 m)
❀❀❀ ◊ ☀

Rubus 'Benenden'
An ornamental blackberry sounds like a contradiction in terms, but this is a beautiful shrub with roselike, pure white flowers from late spring to early summer. The stems are thornless, so pruning—after flowering, if necessary—is not such a pain.

H: 10 ft (3 m); **S**: 10 ft (3 m)
❀❀❀ ◊ ☀

Sarcococca confusa
Christmas box is one of the best of all evergreen shrubs for a shady site, producing highly scented, if rather small, white flowers in the depths of winter among polished, firm, dark green leaves. Plant in quantity for ground cover under deciduous trees.

H: 6 ft (2 m); **S**: 3 ft (1 m)
❀❀❀ ◊ ☀ ☀

Saxifraga 'Tricolor'
A fine foliage plant for shade, this woodland species has kidney-shaped, dark green leaves that are strongly patterned with red and white. Loose panicles of tiny white flowers appear above them in summer. Good in a rock garden or shady border.

H: 12 in (30 cm); **S**: 12 in (30 cm)
❀❀ ◊ ☀ ☀

Saxifraga x urbium
London pride is a robust, evergreen perennial that makes large rosettes of leathery, spoon-shaped, mid-green leaves. Tiny, pink-flushed white flowers stand above them in airy panicles in summer. The plant is valued for its tolerance of dry soil.

H: 12 in (30 cm); **S**: indefinite
❀❀❀ ◊ ☀ ☀

Skimmia x confusa '*Kew Green*'
Skimmias are essential evergreen shrubs, their compact domes making pleasing shapes both in borders and large containers. This hybrid has an abundance of fragrant white spring flowers. They tolerate alkaline soil but are really best in neutral to acidic.

H: up to 10 ft (3 m); **S**: up to 5 ft (1.5 m) ❄❄❄ ◊ ☼ ☀

Smilacina racemosa (*syn.* Maianthemum racemosum)
This plant could easily be mistaken for Solomon's seal, to which it is related, until the fluffy panicles of white flowers appear at the stem tips in spring. These are sometimes followed by green berries that ripen to red.

H: up to 36 in (90 cm); **S**: 24 in (60 cm) ❄❄❄ ◊ ☼ ☀

Symphytum caucasicum
Although this rather coarse plant can be invasive, comfrey is worth considering for its brilliant blue flowers, which are produced over a long period in summer. Some of its hybrids with variegated leaves have less thuggish tendencies.

H: 24 in (60 cm); **S**: 24 in (60 cm) ❄❄❄ ◊ ☼

Tellima grandiflora
Tolerant of dry soil though preferring damper conditions, this perennial produces rosettes of heart-shaped leaves from which erect stems arise, carrying greenish white flowers from late spring to midsummer. 'Perky' is more compact, with red flowers.

H: up to 32 in (80 cm); **S**: 12 in (30 cm) ❄❄❄ ◊ ◑ ☼

Thalictrum aquilegiifolium '*Thundercloud*'
This tall perennial is excellent at the back of a border. Appearing in early summer, the flowers are a fluffy mass of dramatic deep purple on tall slender stems above grayish leaves. It is a plant of considerable distinction.

H: 3 ft (1 m); **S**: 18 in (45 cm) ❄❄❄ ◊ ☼

Tiarella cordifolia
Dainty woodlanders, foam flowers are grown primarily for their lobed leaves, which in the case of this species take on bronze tints when the weather turns colder. The froth of white flowers that floats above them in summer is something of a bonus.

H: 4–12 in (10–30 cm); **S**: 12 in (30 cm) ❄❄❄ ◊ ☼ ☀

Plant guide (Tr–Wi)

Trachelospermum jasminoides

Star jasmine is an evergreen climber with oval, glossy, dark green leaves that benefits from a sheltered spot. The small white flowers appear over a long period from early summer well into fall. The scent is like jasmine but with three times the intensity.

H: 15 ft (5 m); **S**: 10 ft (3 m)
❄❄ ◊ ☀

Trachycarpus fortunei

For a touch of the exotic in cool climates, plant the hardy Chusan palm. Mature specimens have shaggy bark. Use as a focal point in light woodland or in a container, but watch out for the pointed leaves—they can poke your eye out.

H: 6–10 ft (2–3 m); **S**: 6 ft (2 m)
❄❄ ◊ ☀ ☀

Tricyrtis formosana

The toad lily is a graceful little plant for the end of the season. Zigzag stems are topped with lilylike mauve flowers that are heavily spotted with darker mauve. Give them a prominent position so that their quiet charm can be fully appreciated.

H: 32 in (80 cm); **S**: 18 in (45 cm)
❄❄❄ ◊ ☀ ☀

Trillium grandiflorum

Wake robin, a dramatic woodlander, is a desirable spring-flowering perennial, breathtaking where planted *en masse* under deciduous trees but also effective in isolated clumps. It is best appreciated when kept away from daintier flowers.

H: 16 in (40 cm); **S**: 12 in (30 cm)
❄❄❄ ◊ ☀ ☀

Trollius x cultorum '*Orange Princess*'

Globeflowers are useful perennials for shade, flowering from late spring to early summer. Preferring moist soil, they are effective in bog gardens or damp borders. This selection is vigorous, with orange-yellow flowers.

H: 36 in (90 cm); **S**: 18 in (45 cm)
❄❄❄ ◊ ☀

Tropaeolum speciosum

The flame creeper vigorously shoots up from below ground every spring, setting the shadows alight in summer with its brilliant red flowers. It does a wonderful job of enlivening a hedge or large conifer. Nonalkaline soil is essential, preferably cool and damp.

H: 10 ft (3 m) or more; **S**: 3 ft (1 m)
❄❄ ◊ ☀

Viburnum davidii

This low-growing shrub, with shining evergreen leaves, is good at the edge of a border and is effective ground cover. Domed clusters of small white flowers open in spring. To be certain of the blue fall berries, grow plants of both sexes in proximity.

H: 3–5 ft (1–1.5 m); **S**: 3–5 ft (1–1.5 m)
❀❀❀ ◊ ☼

Vinca major 'Variegata'

The variegated form of periwinkle is less invasive than the plain green-leaved species, and has attractive, cream-edged foliage. Blue flowers are scattered among the leaves in spring. Great as ground cover, or use it instead of ivy in containers.

H: 18 in (45 cm); **S**: indefinite
❀❀❀ ◊ ☼ ☀

Vinca minor

The lesser periwinkle is daintier in all its parts than the preceding, and is less vigorous. Recommended for ground cover, it is also an excellent addition to a container or hanging basket. Variegated forms need some sun to maintain good leaf color.

H: 4–8 in (10–20 cm); **S**: indefinite
❀❀❀ ◊ ☼ ☀

Viola labradorica

If it likes you, this innocent-looking little violet will take over the garden, seeding itself where it will. The heart-shaped leaves gleam like burnished bronze. Mauve, but alas, unscented, flowers are held daintily above them in mid- to late spring.

H: 3 in (8 cm); **S**: indefinite
❀❀❀ ◊ ☼

Weigela 'Looymansii Aurea'

Weigelas are reliable shrubs, and this is one of the most attractive, with yellow-green foliage and soft pink flowers in late spring and early summer. It needs just enough sun to bring out the leaf color, with sufficient shade to prevent scorching.

H: 5 ft (1.5 m); **S**: 5 ft (1.5 m)
❀❀❀ ◊ ☼

Wisteria floribunda 'Alba'

For the best flowering, wisterias are usually trained against warm walls, but they thrive in dappled shade, too. They are at their most spectacular when given the support of a mature tree, from which the long racemes drop dramatically in late spring.

H: 28 ft (9 m) or more; **S**: 28 ft (9 m)
❀❀❀ ◊ ☼

Suppliers

Bulbs

Brent & Becky's Bulbs
7900 Daffodil Lane
Gloucester, VA 23061
www.brentandbeckysbulbs.com

Oakes Daylilies
PO Box 268
Corryton, TN 37721
www.oakesdaylilies.com

Old House Gardens
536 Third Street
Ann Arbor, MI 48103
www.oldhousegardens.com

Clematis

Brushwood Nursery
PO Box 483
Unionville, PA 19375
www.gardenvines.com

Silver Star Vinery
31805 NE Clearwater Drive
Yacolt, WA 98675
www.silverstarvinery.com

Hostas

Direct Source Hostas
PO Box 535
Glenview, IL 60025
www.directsourcehostas.com

Made in the Shade Gardens
16370 W. 138th Terrace
Olathe, KS 66062
www.hostaguy.com

Ivies and ferns

Classy Groundcovers
PO Box 2556
Blairsville, GA 30514
www.classygroundcovers. com

ECOLAGE
2623 West Sale Road
Lake Charles, LA 70605
www.ecolage.safeshopper.com

Perennials

Bluestone Perennials
7211 Middle Ridge Road
Madison, OH 44057
www.bluestoneperennials.com

Garden Crossings LLC
4902 96th Avenue
Zeeland, MI 49464
www.gardencrossings.com

Plant Delights Nursery
9241 Sauls Road
Raleigh, NC 27603
www.plantdelights.com

Roses

Antique Rose Emporium
9300 Lueckemeyer Road
Brenham, TX 77833
www.antiqueroseemporium.com

Chamblee's Rose Nursery
10926 U.S. Hwy. 69 North
Tyler, TX 75706
www.chambleeroses.com

David Austin Roses Limited
15059 State Hwy. 64 West
Tyler, TX 75704
www.davidaustinroses.com

Trees & shrubs

Forestfarm
990 Tetherow Road
Williams, OR 97544
www.forestfarm.com

St. Lawrence Nurseries
325 State Highway 345
Potsdam, NY 13676
www.sln.potsdam.ny.us

Cutting & hand tools

Lee Valley Tools, Ltd.
P.O. Box 6295, Station J
Ottawa, Ontario K2A 1T4
www.leevalley.com

Garden ornaments

Gardener's Supply Company
128 Intervale Road
Burlington, VT 05401
www.gardeners.com

Seeds

Johnny's Selected Seeds
955 Benton Avenue
Winslow, ME 04901
www.johnnyseeds.com

Swallowtail Garden Seeds
122 Calistoga Road #178
Santa Rosa, CA 95409
www.swallowtailgardenseeds.com

Trellises & supports

Plow & Hearth
PO Box 6000
Madison, VA 22727
www.plowhearth.com

Water plants & features

Lilypons Water Gardens
6800 Lilypons Road
Adamstown, MD 21710
www.lilypons.com

Index

Index

Acknowledgments

The publisher would like to thank the following for their kind permission to reproduce their photographs

(Key: a-above; b-below/bottom; c-center; l-left; r-right; t-top)

6-7 DK Images: Peter Anderson, designer: Nick Williams-Ellis/The Jurassic Coast Garden/Chelsea Flower Show 2006. **8** DK Images: Steve Wooster/Designer: Phil Jaffa, Chelsea Flower Show 2004 (tr). Andrew Lawson: (br). **9** Leigh Clapp: Culverkeys. **11** Marianne Majerus Photography: Designer: Michele Osborne (t); DK Images, Peter Anderson; Designers: Diane Appleyard, Paul Ashton, Dawn Johnson, Simon Street, John Walker/ A garden for Robin/Chelsea Flower Show 2006. **13** Brian T. North: Designer: Zia Allaway. **14-15** Andrew Lawson. **18** DK Images, Peter Anderson; designers: The Pantiles Design Centre/ The Blue Garden/

Hampton Court Flower Show 2006 (t); DK Images: Peter Anderson, designer: Nick Williams-Ellis/The Jurassic Coast Garden/Chelsea Flower Show 2006 (b). **22-23** DK Images: Peter Anderson; designer: Tom Hoblyn/The Artist's Garden/Hampton Court Flower Show 2006. **24** www. cuprinol.co.uk: (br). **25** DK Images: Peter Anderson; designer Annie Konig/The Weleda Garden/Hampton Court Flower Show 2006. **26** DK Images: Peter Anderson; designer: Tom Hoblyn/The Artist's Garden/Hampton Court Flower Show 2006. **27** DK Images: Peter Anderson; Coton Manor Garden (bl); designer Alison Sloga/ Immaculate Square Garden/Hampton Court Flower Show 2006. **29** DK Images: Peter Anderson; designers: Marcus Barnett and Philip Nixon/Savills Garden, Chelsea Flower Show 2006. **30** DK Images: Emma Firth. **43 27** DK Images: Peter Anderson; Coton

Manor Garden **46** S & O Mathews Photography: The Little Cottage, Lymington. **49** John Glover: Bransford Nursery, Worcs (br). **91** Garden Picture Library: Botanica. **93** Marianne Majerus Photography: Beth Chatto's Garden, Essex. **103** Photos Horticultural. **115** FLPA: Nigel Cattlin (tr); RHS Wisley (br). **116** DK Images: Peter Anderson (l). **117** Science Photo Library: Geoff Kidd (bl); RHS Wisley (tr). **122-3** DK Images: Peter Anderson; Coton Manor Garden

All other images © Dorling Kindersley

For further information, see www.dkimages.com

Dorling Kindersley would also like to thank the following: Neal's Nurseries for prop loans; Coton Manor Garden (www.cotonmanor.co.uk) for locations.